THE WAY PEOPLE LIVE

Life in a Medieval Village

Titles in The Way People Live series include:

Cowboys in the Old West
Games of Ancient Rome
Life Aboard the Space Shuttle
Life Among the Great Plains Indians
Life Among the Ibo Women of Nigeria
Life Among the Pirates
Life Among the Samurai
Life Among the Vikings
Life During the American Revolution
Life During the Black Death
Life During the Crusades
Life During the Gold Rush
Life During the Great Depression
Life During the Middle Ages
Life During the Renaissance
Life During the Roaring Twenties
Life During the Russian Revolution
Life During the Spanish Inquisition
Life in a Japanese American Internment
    Camp
Life in a Medieval Castle
Life in a Medieval Monastery
Life in a Nazi Concentration Camp
Life in a Wild West Show
Life in America During the 1960s
Life in an Amish Community
Life in Ancient Athens
Life in Ancient China
Life in Ancient Egypt
Life in Ancient Greece

Life in Ancient Rome
Life in Berlin
Life in Charles Dickens's England
Life in Communist Russia
Life in Genghis Khan's Mongolia
Life in Hong Kong
Life in Moscow
Life in Tokyo
Life in War-Torn Bosnia
Life in the Amazon Rain Forest
Life in the American Colonies
Life in the Australian Outback
Life in the Elizabethan Theater
Life in the Hitler Youth
Life in the North During the Civil War
Life in the South During the Civil War
Life of a Medieval Knight
Life of a Nazi Soldier
Life of a Roman Slave
Life of a Roman Soldier
Life of a Slave on a Southern Plantation
Life on Alcatraz
Life on Ellis Island
Life on an African Slave Ship
Life on an Everest Expedition
Life on the American Frontier
Life on the Oregon Trail
Life on the Pony Express
Life on the Underground Railroad
Life Under the Jim Crow Laws

THE WAY
PEOPLE
LIVE

Life in a Medieval Village

by
James Barter

LUCENT
BOOKS ®

THOMSON
✦
GALE

San Diego • Detroit • New York • San Francisco • Cleveland • New Haven, Conn. • Waterville, Maine • London • Munich

On cover: A painting by Pieter Brueghel
entitled *Village Wedding.*

LIBRARY OF CONGRESS CATALOGING-IN-PUBLICATION DATA

Barter, James, 1946–
    Life in a medieval village / by James Barter.
        p. cm. — (The way people live)
    Includes bibliographical references and index.
        ISBN 1-59018-266-9
        1. Cities and towns, Medieval—Juvenile literature. 2. Civilization, Medieval—Juvenile
    literature. 3. Europe—Social life and customs—Juvenile literature. 4. Middle Ages—
    Juvenile literature. I. Title. II. Series.

    GT120 .B37 2003
    307.76'094'0902—dc21

                                                                      2002152875

Printed in the United States of America

Contents

FOREWORD
Discovering the Humanity in Us All   6

INTRODUCTION
The Emergence of the Medieval Village   8

CHAPTER ONE
The Village Manor House—
Lives of the Nobility   14

CHAPTER TWO
The Village Workers   25

CHAPTER THREE
A Calendar of Toil   36

CHAPTER FOUR
Family Life in the Cottage   46

CHAPTER FIVE
Marriage and the Family   56

CHAPTER SIX
Relaxation and Enjoyment   66

CHAPTER SEVEN
Village Justice   76

Notes   85
For Further Reading   88
Works Consulted   89
Index   92
Picture Credits   95
About the Author   96

Discovering the Humanity in Us All

Books in The Way People Live series focus on groups of people in a wide variety of circumstances, settings, and time periods. Some books focus on different cultural groups, others on people in a particular historical time period, while others cover people involved in a specific event. Each book emphasizes the daily routines, personal and historical struggles, and achievements of people from all walks of life.

To really understand any culture, it is necessary to strip the mind of the common notions we hold about groups of people. These stereotypes are the archenemies of learning. It does not even matter whether the stereotypes are positive or negative; they are confining and tight. Removing them is a challenge that's not easily met, as anyone who has ever tried it will admit. Ideas that do not fit into the templates we create are unwelcome visitors—ones we would prefer remain quietly in a corner or forgotten room.

The cowboy of the Old West is a good example of such confining roles. The cowboy was courageous, yet soft-spoken. His time (it is always a he in our template) was spent alternatively saving a rancher's daughter from certain death on a runaway stagecoach or shooting it out with rustlers. At times, of course, he was likely to get a little crazy in town after a trail drive, but for the most part he was the epitome of inner strength. It is disconcerting to find out that the cowboy is human, even a bit childish. Can it really be true that cowboys would line up to help the cook on the trail drive grind coffee, just hoping he would give them a little stick of peppermint candy that came with the coffee shipment? The idea of tough cowboys vying with one another to help "Coosie" (as they called their cooks) for a bit of candy seems silly and out of place.

So is the vision of Eskimos playing video games and watching MTV, living in prefab housing in the Arctic. It just does not fit with what "Eskimo" means. We are far more comfortable with snow igloos and whale blubber, harpoons and kayaks.

Although the cultures dealt with in Lucent's The Way People Live series are often historically and socially well known, the emphasis is on the personal aspects of life. Groups of people, while unquestionably affected by their politics and their governmental structures, are more than those institutions. How do people in a particular time and place educate their children? What do they eat? And how do they build their houses? What kinds of work do they do? What kinds of games do they enjoy? The answers to these questions bring these cultures to life. People's lives are revealed in the particulars and only by knowing the particulars can we understand these cultures' will to survive and their moments of weakness and greatness.

This is not to say that understanding politics does not help to understand a culture. There is no question that the Warsaw ghetto, for example, was a culture that was brought about by the politics and social ideas of Adolf

Hitler and the Third Reich. But the Jews who were crowded together in the ghetto cannot be understood by the Reich's politics. Their life was a day-to-day battle for existence, and the creativity and methods they used to prolong their lives is a vital story of human perseverance that would be denied by focusing only on the institutions of Hitler's Germany. Knowing that children as young as five or six outwitted Nazi guards on a daily basis, that Jewish policemen helped the Germans control the ghetto, that children attended secret schools in the ghetto and even earned diplomas— these are the things that reveal the fabric of life, that can inspire, intrigue, and amaze.

Books in The Way People Live series allow both the casual reader and the student to see humans as victims, heroes, and onlookers. And although humans act in ways that can fill us with feelings of sorrow and revulsion, it is important to remember that "hero," "predator," and "victim" are dangerous terms. Heaping undue pity or praise on people reduces them to objects and strips them of their humanity.

Seeing the Jews of Warsaw only as victims is to deny their humanity. Seeing them only as they appear in surviving photos, staring at the camera with infinite sadness, is limiting, both to them and to those who want to understand them. To an object of pity the only appropriate response becomes "Those poor creatures!" and that reduces both the quality of their struggle and the depth of their despair. No one is served by such two-dimensional views of people and their cultures.

With this in mind, The Way People Live series strives to flesh out the traditional, two-dimensional views of people in various cultures and historical circumstances. Using a wide variety of primary quotations—the words not only of the politicians and government leaders but of the real people whose lives are being examined—each book in the series attempts to show an honest and complete picture of a culture removed from our own by time or space.

By examining cultures in this way, the reader will notice not only the glaring differences from his or her own culture but also will be struck by the similarities. For indeed, people share common needs—warmth, good company, stability, and affirmation from others. Ultimately, seeing how people really live, or have lived, can only enrich our understanding of ourselves.

The Emergence of the Medieval Village

The Middle Ages occurred in Europe between the end of the Roman Empire, about A.D. 500, and the beginning of the Renaissance, around 1400. The phrase *Middle Ages* was first used by fifteenth-century scholars to describe the middle period between the ancient time of the Roman Empire and their modern era.

Historians have difficulty agreeing on what made that nine-hundred-year era unique. Generally, however, they agree that this period was a time when people throughout much of Europe lost the protection and stability provided by the Roman Empire and sought safety and defense in small communities centered around a lord or a master. Most of theses villages were isolated from each other, with occasional visits from peddlers, priests, soldiers, and neighboring villagers. Ninety percent of Europe's medieval population lived sheltered and isolated in small rural villages far from urban centers such as Rome, Paris, London, and Cologne. During this period such capital cities were much like their kings and royal families—far away, inaccessible, and rarely if ever visited by villagers.

Each of thousands of medieval villages was dependent only upon itself. Each was the only community its population relied upon for all of life's needs. Each was where people

A fourteenth-century engraving depicts a bustling medieval village.

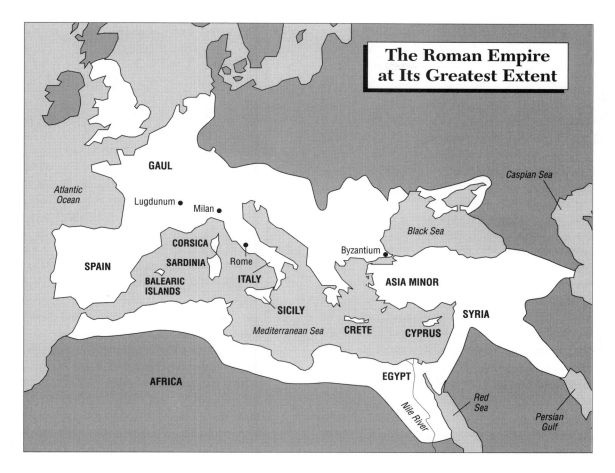

The Roman Empire at Its Greatest Extent

lived, worked, socialized, married, enjoyed local festivals, drank ale, attended church, violated village laws, gave birth to children, quarreled and fought, got sick, and eventually died. Ideas about the world beyond the village existed, to be certain, but most villagers rarely strayed more than a day's walk away. Birth, childhood, work, marriage, and death occurred within a ten-mile radius.

Roman Dominance and Failure

Historians are nearly unanimous in their view that the collapse of the Roman Empire was the most significant event that triggered the rise of tens of thousands of medieval villages. Prior to the collapse, all villages and cities fell within the hegemony of Rome. As the final authority in all matters, Rome extended considerable clout as well as security across the European landscape. The unity that Rome brought included one common language, the protection of Roman legions, Roman law, and a common currency that created a healthy economy among all members of the empire.

Citizens of the empire had never experienced greater security and prosperity. The early third-century Roman writer Tertullian, while visiting the farms and villages throughout Roman Europe, made this admiring observation:

Delightful farms have now blotted out every trace of the dreadful wastes; cultivated fields have supplanted woods; flocks and herds have driven out wild beasts; sandy spots are sewn; rocks and stones have been cleared away; bogs have been drained. Large villages now occupy land hardly tenanted before by cottages. Thick population meets the eye on all sides.[1]

The Roman Empire, however successful, was not destined to last forever. When the collapse occurred, spurred along by repeated invasions by Germanic tribes, the security, safety, and prosperity that European villagers had enjoyed quickly vanished. No other empire or institution existed that could step in and replace the Roman Empire. Contrary to Tertullian's poetic description of third-century village life, Paul the Deacon, a seventh-century French historian, depicted the countryside after the fall of Rome with this very different description:

> The flocks remain alone in the pastures. You saw villas or fortified places filled with people in utter silence. The whole world seemed brought to its ancient stillness: no voice in the field, no whistling of shepherds. The harvests were untouched. Human habitations became the abode of wild beasts.[2]

Retrenchment and Fear

The unity and quality of life that Europe had enjoyed under the Roman Empire lay shattered. Law and order, the twin pillars that had supported and promoted the success of thousands of towns and villages, collapsed.

Without the Roman legions and courts, all were at the mercy of chaos. Roving bands of unemployed and homeless poor people wandered the countryside, living in camps along the roads. Unable to find work to pay for their food and clothing, they robbed villagers and travelers in order to survive. Farmers and craftsmen soon found themselves neglecting their businesses in order to protect their families and homes. Unable to pay their taxes, many farmers were forced to sell their oxen or even their land. Stripped of the central authority of the Roman Empire, the countryside suffered a severe and relatively quick decline. In the words of historians Jean Chapelot and Robert Fossier in their book *The Village and House in the Middle Ages,* the villages became

> ill-defined, full of shadows and contrasts, isolated and unorganized islands of cultivation, patches of uncertain authority, shattered family groupings around a patriarch, a chieftain, or a rich man . . . a landscape still in a state of anarchy, in short, the picture of a world that man seemed unable to control or dominate.[3]

The Bond of Lords and Peasants

Villagers able to survive amid this crisis recognized that their most immediate need was protection. Desperate to reestablish some semblance of economic stability and personal security, frightened villagers sought the assistance of wealthy landowners. Their reasoning was simple: Wealthy landowners, who could afford to build large stone homes and to arm themselves on horseback with swords and armor, would be capable of defending them from marauding bands of thieves and robbers. Such protection would then free the villagers to return to their primary job of working in fields and shops to support their families.

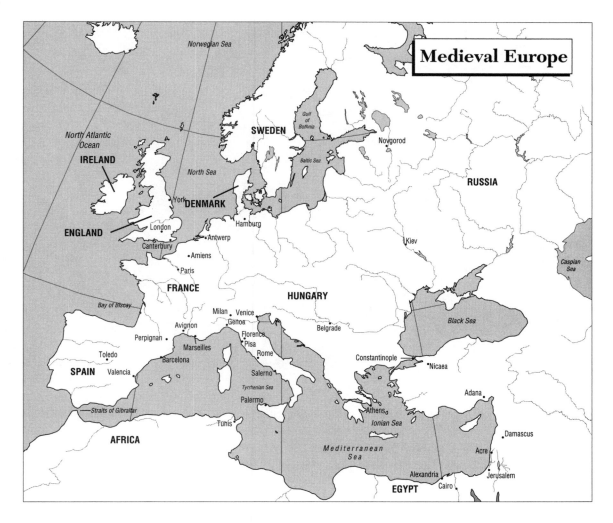

Lords were more than willing to provide military protection. During the seventh and eighth centuries, the villages of the European countryside gradually were built near large stone manor houses; in some few cases, they grew around walled manor houses or castles. In times of extreme danger, all villagers fled to the protection of the manor house or castle to participate in its defense along with the lord and his family.

Villagers paid a stiff price for their security. In return for the lord's protection, all village members pledged to work for the lord or to reimburse him in one of many ways. In exchange for a small plot of farmland to feed their families, some desperate farmers agreed to give a portion of their crop to the lord as rent. Others working the lord's land agreed to pay him with services, such as providing menial labor in the manor house cleaning, cooking, or making repairs once or twice a week. Craftsmen paid their dues as well. They pledged to provide goods to the lord such as bread, milled flour, or butchered beef either at an annual rate or whenever the lord demanded it.

The Emergence of the Medieval Village

A painting shows a flurry of activity surrounding the lives of medieval villagers, each engaged in a unique function that served to improve the village community.

Trading goods and services for the lord's protection initially benefited both groups. Over time, however, this system gradually strengthened the authority of the lords, who became increasingly powerful and affluent while the villagers became increasingly poor, distraught, and enslaved. *"Omnes homines aut liberi sunt aut sevrvi,"*[4] proclaimed the thirteenth-century French jurist Henry de Bracton in Latin. This meant, "All men are either free or servile." Thus, he correctly observed that all of medieval humanity was divisible into two groups that generally defined the social structure of the medieval village. With very few exceptions, the only *liberi,* or free villagers, were the lord and his extended family. All others, all 90 percent or more, fell into the great mass of the *servi.*

The self-reliance of each village and the relationship between the *liberi* and the *servi* were only two of the characteristics of a medieval village. It was also defined by its many geographical properties. To function successfully, villages required favorable locations with reasonably mild climates, a reasonable population size, and plenty of natural resources.

The Characteristics of Medieval Villages

Of the tens of thousands of villages in Europe, no two were alike. Each was unique in size, shape, abundance of natural resources, arable acreage, forests, meadows, population, and number of structures. Yet within such diversity emerges a general mosaic of the medieval village that depicts a verdant landscape with lush, rolling grain fields; a sparkling cold-water river; thick forests populated with a variety of wild game and timber; meadows suitable for grazing livestock; and different types of man-made structures that housed and supported the villagers' ways of life.

Size and population varied considerably. Small villages might have had as few as fifty residents covering no more than two square miles. In 1279 the fairly modest manor and village of Alwalton, England, was described in this way for the tax records:

> The court of the said manor with its garden contains one half an acre. And to the whole of the said vill [village] of Alwalton belong 5 hides and a half and 1 virgate of land and a half; of which each hide contains 5 virgates of land and each virgate contains 25 acres.[5]

Larger villages, with populations of six or seven hundred, could spread out across twenty square miles.

The feature that most defined the medieval village was its site. Whether located along the coast close to good fishing grounds, high in the alpine mountains where the abundance of forests drove the local economies, or along a verdant low-lying river valley rich with fertile black soil and grazing meadows, everyone had to adapt their lives to what the village geography had to offer.

The Site

Survival as an independent village required a site capable of supporting the needs of all villagers. Of all natural resources necessary for a varied economy, water was the most important. For this reason, villages were always established along a river or a stream. Water was used to irrigate fields, drive waterwheels that in turn milled flour, improve pasture land for grazing livestock, move goods to other villages, provide a source of food, and function as the village sewer system.

Another important consideration was the proximity of a site to building materials, both stone and wood. Stone was the most desired building material for permanent large structures such as the manor house for the lord's family, the parish church, and utilitarian structures such as bridges, mills, and bell towers. Wood taken from a local forest had value for the homes and cottages of the village peasants. Wood was also essential for everyone's evening fire for cooking and heating. In addition to the use of forests for lumber, they also provided a habitat for animals such as deer, wild boars, bears, river otters, rabbits, and a variety of fowl, all of which were important sources of meat in the medieval kitchen.

Natural defense was also an important consideration. Unlike major cities such as Paris, London, Rome, and Florence, which were large enough to construct their own defense walls, villages had to fend for themselves. The next-best alternative was to position part of a village on some high ground that forced attackers to struggle uphill. High ground also afforded an excellent lookout position for viewing the surrounding lands for potential trouble. Often the highest ground was also the place of the village manor house. Always the most imposing house in the village, it stood as the lord's family home and as a place of central authority and defense for the villagers.

The Village Manor House—Lives of the Nobility

The manor house was the most visible symbol of the lord's lofty status and absolute authority over the village. Often the largest stone structure in the village, the manor house served a variety of functions. It was the personal residence of the lord and his family, the place where the lord conducted business and held court, a place of entertainment for other visiting lords, and sometimes the center of various village activities. Whichever function the manor house was fulfilling at any time, it was always a busy place.

Many symbols of wealth could be found inside the large manor house, and none was more evident than the household staff of servants. Wealthy, powerful lords had many servants who kept track of their holdings, ran the manor house, and took care of the needs of the family members. Each day the manor house was filled with the noise and energy of a large staff, some of whom lived in servants' quarters at the manor house and others who arrived early each morning from the village.

The Day Begins

The lord's family was well cared for. It was typically the only family that enjoyed assistance to maintain its house and to serve its needs. Each day, a staff of servants larger than the family itself moved throughout the manor house performing all of the necessary daily activities, including cleaning, cooking,

making repairs, caring for horses, and attending to the children.

The day usually began before sunrise and before the family rose. Servants started the morning with baking, chopping wood to heat the house, drawing water, and readying the horses. Once the lord and his lady had arisen, chambermaids ventured into their room, swept floors, emptied chamber pots, and filled their wash basins with warm water; meanwhile, the laundress gathered together any dirty clothes to begin the day's wash. For their part, the lord and lady of the castle made sure they were tidy before they greeted their household or any guests by washing with warm water from their basins while partially clothed to keep warm.

A small breakfast of bread and a drink of milk, buttermilk, or herbs steeped in warm water was taken by all the family, including the children. After breakfast the lord and his family might enter a small private chapel for morning mass. Once mass was complete, the family went about its daily routine; the lord tackled the day's business, the lady managed the house staff, and small children were educated by their mother and perhaps tutors.

As the royal family departed for their daily affairs, the house staff went to work addressing all of the needs of the family. Walls, and the painted canvases that covered them to keep out drafts, required constant cleaning to remove the dirt and soot that came from the central open fireplace. Farm equipment, bows, swords, and spears were repaired,

A fifteenth-century manuscipt illumination shows a lord and lady expressing affection for their children in the hall of their village manor house.

cleaned, and properly stored. Horses also needed provisioning and shoeing, and repairs were made to riding equipment.

Each morning villagers headed up the hill to the manor house to deliver the day's supply of fresh breads, meats, fish, foul, and wine. During the winter a plentiful supply of wood was also brought to the manor to keep the house as warm as possible and to fuel the kitchen fires.

A staff of cooks baked early in the morning. Bread was made by the village baker, but all other food was prepared in the manor house. Cooks placed large pieces of meat or fowl on the kitchen spit and basted them with long wooden spoons while they rotated. A side of beef or a whole pig slow roasted for up to six hours. Other cooks received cheese and butter as payment from the local peasants and prepared them for the midday meal along with vegetables, fruits, and desserts.

Following the evening meal, the kitchen was cleaned and all cookware put away. Not long after dark, the family retired for the night. The members of the family found a good night's sleep on comfortable mattresses, and although they did not have fireplaces in their bedrooms, goose-down blankets kept them warm. A night of rest was important, especially for the lord and lady, because each

The Pilgrimage

The medieval church encouraged as many people as possible to make long journeys, called pilgrimages, to religious shrines throughout Europe.

Although medieval pilgrimages were not intended to be just for the wealthy and educated classes, few outside of the nobility had the money or the time to make a pilgrimage, which might take two weeks at a minimum and up to three months if they chose to walk. Anyone who went on such a journey, regardless of income, placed the operations of home, fields, livestock, and business at risk.

Some people believed that such pilgrimages showed penance for sins they had committed and would win them forgiveness from God. Others went on pilgrimages as acts of thanksgiving for some good fortune they had received or after recovery from a life-threatening disease. The most visited destinations were Jerusalem; Rome; Santiago de Compostela, Spain; La Mont-Saint-Michel, France; and Canterbury, England.

The value of the pilgrimage for the most devout pilgrims was the suffering experienced along the way. These pilgrims, although a minority, believed that by suffering they were demonstrating to God the sincerity of their religious commitment. Some took the pilgrimage so seriously that they wore their coarsest clothing so that it scratched and chafed their skin. Some even traveled the entire journey barefoot, carrying a staff to assist them when they became lame. The more they suffered, they believed, the greater the likelihood that God would look favorably upon their lives.

Some business people benefited financially from the pilgrims, particularly hoteliers and tavern, shop, and ship owners. There were also the sellers of souvenirs and pilgrim badges along the routes. Pilgrims who either could not or chose not to go any farther bought items from them. With the badges and souvenirs in hand, they returned to their towns and villages claiming to have proof of their visits. Some even returned home having purchased pieces of paper granting them pardons and forgiveness for their sins and assurance of a place in heaven.

had a full day of obligations to discharge beginning early in the morning.

The Lord

Of paramount importance to the villagers was the lord's obligation to provide for the village's protection. It was his duty to provide a safe haven for the villagers in the event of an invasion. This role was always displayed by the lord as he rode his horse with his sword strapped to his waist. According to historian Norman Cantor in his book *The Medieval Reader,*

Whatever else the aristocracy did—in politics, religion, art, and literature—it was military valor and personal strength and courage that had originally made the great noble families powerful in society, and this physical prowess was continually necessary to sustain their position in society.[6]

This obligation meant the lord and his male family members had to practice defending the village. The lord and his family were obligated to provide mounted horsemen in full armor for the defense of the village, so they practiced jousting on horseback with long lances. They also honed their fencing and archery skills. This obligation was viewed as having the strength of a contract, and for that reason the lord of a village often pledged an oath to each subject, such as this one from the thirteenth century that promises to provide protection:

It is right that those who offer to us unbroken fidelity [faithful service] should be protected by our aid. And since such and such a faithful one of ours, by the favor of God, coming here in our palace, we willing bear arms for those who has seen fit to swear trust and fidelity to us in our hand, therefore we decree and command by the present precept that for the future this yeoman be counted with the number of antrustions [loyal followers who were protected].[7]

In his role as the financial leader of the village, the lord rented land and buildings to the villagers, who worked them to generate their personal incomes. On a daily basis, or whenever it became necessary, the lord sat with his financial manager, called the steward, and reviewed rents paid as well as debts owed to him. This was the fundamental nature of the village economy, and it was in everyone's interest to keep it balanced.

The lord's third principal obligation was to oversee the village laws and their enforcement. The lord was present whenever cases needed to be heard. Generally the proceedings took place outside the manor house at an established place marked by a large tree or a bridge. After hearing both sides of a case, it was the lord's responsibility either to acquit the accused person or to impose penalties ranging from fines to brutal physical tortures. The lord's authority was rarely challenged.

This fifteenth-century painting shows lords and ladies fishing. The nobility engaged in outdoor recreation to provide a reprieve from their obligations to the village.

Varied Livestock

The uniqueness of each medieval village was partly defined by its resources. Livestock, for example, played a key role in the agrarian economy of each village, providing food and employing labor; yet its ubiquitous presence belies its diversity from village to village. In fifteenth-century Wiltshire, England, more than 90 percent of the villagers owned some sort of farm animal, primarily cows and sheep, yet in Taunton, England, that number was just 60 percent. In Doullens, France, at this same time, 80 percent of the small farmers owned sheep but no cattle, yet only twenty miles away, in Albert, farmers preferred raising pigs. In Germany, records indicate that in the village of Daun, horses were used by 85 percent of the farmers for plowing their fields; in Keusel, oxen were prevalent, and no horse appears on the tax rolls.

A medieval family tends to their livestock. Livestock were an important component of the village economy.

In addition to the lord's legal responsibilities, he also owed military allegiance to the king that sometimes absented him from the village. Under such circumstance, he appointed a handful of men to assist him in the administration of the village. Good advice in this regard was given during the thirteenth century by the writer Walter of Henley, who admonished all lords, "Look into your affairs often, and cause them to be reviewed, for those who serve you will thereby avoid the more to do wrong."[8] This was wise counsel because an absent lord needed the loyal and honest assistance of several officials to oversee the village in his absence.

The broad obligations on the part of the lord for administering the affairs of the village extended everywhere except for the manor house. This was the one domain under the control of his wife, the manorial lady. Her principal job included overseeing all of the activities within the manor house, which ranged from meals and royal visitors to assuming the duties of her husband in times of war.

The Lady

Bearing children was the principal duty of the lady of the manor. The need for as many sons as possible to assist the lord in the defense of the village sometimes meant families had six to eight children of both sexes. Once this responsibility was discharged, usually by the time she was in mid to late twenties, the lady took charge of the entire manor house. She oversaw the cooking and cleaning, made menus for meals, and kept financial accounts. She was in charge of entertaining guests that arrived and remained at the manor for as long as a week or more while at the same time providing an education for her children.

Servants kept the manor maintained, but the lady of the manor still had much to do every day to ensure that the household ran smoothly. Although medieval noblewomen enjoyed spending some of their time in leisurely activities, such as needlework and playing an instrument, their principal responsibilities were to oversee the household and raise the children. Modern medieval historian Sherrilyn Kenyon describes a day in the life of a noblewoman in this way:

> An average day for a noblewoman might include attending morning mass, grabbing a quick bite to break the fast, meeting with servants to instruct them on special duties for the day, meeting with the steward and other officials, overlooking accounts and records, and breaking for the midday meal at noon. If guests were present, she'd spend the rest of the day entertaining them with hunting trips, hawking, singing, or some other planned festivity. Otherwise she'd check on the servants, and make sure the children were attending their lessons. In the absence of her husband, she would also be expected to hear complaints and even rule in legal matters. In the event of attack she would lead the manor's defense.[9]

The lady also needed to be able to take decisive action. In times of crisis, when the lord and his warriors were away on the battlefield,

In their spare time, village noblewomen often engaged in spinning wool for the making of cloth.

the lady took over jobs that the lord normally fulfilled. Governing in her husband's name, the lady engaged in legal transactions, oversaw agricultural activities, and collected rents. On rare occasions, she even needed to be able to defend her estate against sieges or to lead armies on the battlefield.

Noblewomen also provided a counterbalance to warfare and hunting. They encouraged poetry and other literary arts and were more likely to read and write Latin than their husbands. A lady was also the one who was in charge of supervising the education of her children and training the young girls living in the manor about cooking, spinning, embroidering, and medicine. Although the day-to-day duties of the lady of the manor might be tightly constrained, she nevertheless exercised considerable influence over her family and occasionally the village in general.

No single event in the manor house was more time consuming and complicated than major meals, especially those served for many visiting royalty. Such meals were the major social events of the year, and the lady of the manor worked with her staff for weeks to ensure a successful event.

Meals

The finest foods were reserved for guests visiting the manor. The long distances that nobility often traveled to visit meant staying for several days before returning home. An entourage of several lords and ladies meant large gatherings at mealtimes. Meats consisted of fresh kill from the lord's forest of deer, wild boars, pheasants, geese, and swans. Exotic spices imported from India and Asia, such as clove, cinnamon, pepper, and cardamom, were used by the nobility to add flavor to the meats. A variety of local vegetables were given to the lord by villagers who owed them as part of their obligation in exchange for the use of the lord's lands. Fresh fruits from local orchards—apples, pears, plums, and peaches—were supplemented by wild fruits and nuts from the lord's forest. For dessert, honey from the local beekeeper smothered the fruit. In addition to these local products, there were imported luxuries such as sugar (including a special kind made with roses and violets), rice, almonds, figs, dates, raisins, oranges, and pomegranates purchased in town or at fairs.

At the major meal of the day, eaten between 11:00 A.M. and 1:00 P.M., servants set up several long trestle tables in the great hall, the largest room in the manor, and spread large tablecloths that hung down to the floor. Such long tablecloths were used as napkins by the guests and were changed after each course. Servants then set the table with iron knives, silver spoons, dishes for salt, silver cups, and mazers, which were shallow silver-rimmed wooden bowls. At each place was a trencher, a thick slice of day-old bread that served as a plate for the roast meat.

Meals were announced by a horn blown to signal time for washing hands. Servants with pitchers of water, basins, and towels assisted the guests. At the tables, seating followed status: The most important guests were at the high table—the table set apart from and in front of all the others—with the central places reserved for the lord and his family followed by the parish priest and any visiting dignitaries. After grace, the procession of servants bearing food began. First came the bread and butter, followed by the wine or locally brewed ale, and finally the meats and vegetables. Chunks of meat were eaten with the hands and a knife while soups were drunk directly from wooden bowls. Much to the objection of the lady of the

Dining Etiquette

Using proper dining etiquette was an important ingredient to a pleasurable meal in the manor house. Although most food was eaten with the fingers, bigger pieces of meat required a knife but never a fork. The food was always taken from the serving plate, placed on a trencher, and then eaten. Historian Anthony Viscount Montague notes some of the rules, which are included in the *Sussex Archaeological Collections:*

- Let no one take food until the blessing be given, nor take a seat, except that which the master of the house chooses.
- Never take up food with hands not washed.
- Let your finger nails be trimmed.
- Do not press the cheese and the butter on to your bread with the thumb.

- Let not the piece of food, when it has been touched by the teeth, be put back upon the serving dish.
- Do not scratch your limb, after the fashion of a mole, as you sit down, nor pick thy nose.
- Let not persons eating, clean their teeth with their knife.
- Don't spit over the table, nor down upon it ever.
- If you can, don't belch at table.
- Let not a cat ever be a companion to you at the table.
- Wipe your knife, and wipe your spoon with your napkin.
- Put not your knife on your trenchers lest you be reproved.
- Do not chew visibly on either side of the jaw.

manor, men enjoyed throwing bits of meat and bones to the dogs under the table.

Following a long meal, guests and family retired from the great hall to allow servants to clear and put away the table, wash the dishes, rebuild the fire, and spend the rest of the day cleaning and making the manor ready for the next day. It was usually at this time, when the house staff was occupied and guests were resting after their long meal, that the lady found time to be with her children. She would often read to them and teach them the family traditions because one day they would head their own households.

Children

The children of the nobility were raised to become lords and ladies themselves. For this

reason, they began to train for their future roles at an early age. From a young age, children were cared for by their mother and a nanny. The household servants helped to rear the children as well. Until boys were eight, they were usually under their mother's supervision, learning basic life on the estate. Girls continued under their mother's care until they were married, which could be any time between ages twelve and eighteen.

Children of nobility were raised to make quick and decisive decisions. They played simple games that tested their physical capabilities, such as games involving accurately throwing rocks and horseshoes, playful dueling with wooden swords, jousting with long poles, swimming, and, during the winter, tying horse bones to their shoes and skating on frozen ponds. Both boys and girls also played games that developed thinking skills

A fourteenth-century painting shows three noble children. Noble children were raised to be able to eventually take over the duties of the village lords and ladies.

and strategies. Popular indoor games on rainy days included various dice and card games, checkers, and, for older children, the more complex game of chess.

When the lord's sons, whose title was usually that of a knight, were eight years old, they were sent away to a nearby manor of a friend or relative to work as a page, a young knight in training. This exchange of boys within the nobility was believed to produce independent soldiers and to provide an opportunity for boys to meet and form loyalties with other noble families. During this time, they learned the skills required of all knights. They learned the basic manners of the nobility, all the tasks around the manor house, caring for horses, local geography, simple arithmetic, and a few Latin verses. When the young page turned twelve or thirteen, he was made a squire, and his education intensified.

Winning His Spurs

The firstborn son of a lord was always the most important child in the household and to the village. He would one day become a knight like his father, and he would become the sole son to inherit all of his father's land. The responsibilities that a squire would inherit demanded that his education be taken seriously and completed in a thorough and proper manner.

Most important to the squire's studies was gaining military experience. While wearing armor, he practiced jumping ditches, climbing walls, and vaulting into the saddle of his horse. Armed with various kinds of heavy swords, he strengthened his arms by slashing wood posts and various types of moving objects. In addition to this sort of training, he became an expert shot with the bow and arrow. He also learned how to throw the war hammer and the battle-ax. Most important, he practiced fighting while mounted on his horse. This involved thrusting his lance at full speed. This part of his education was made fun by practicing his horsemanship skills hunting deer and wild boars with his lance.

As a knight, his horse would be the most significant instrument of warfare. Much of his training included the care of horses, not only how to groom them but also how to stable, feed, and care for them when they became ill. The squire also needed to learn how to place armor on his horse and how to give direction to his horse for turning, stopping, changing speed, charging straight ahead, and stopping with the use of his feet alone.

Becoming a knight involved more than preparing for war. He would also be required to manage his own manor house one day, and part of his education applied to manners that he would be expected to display. He needed to learn how to cut bread and pass it using the pointed end of the bread knife, to pour wine neatly, to understand the different cuts of meat, and how to correctly carve carcasses. He also needed to learn how to gracefully receive his peers as well as his superiors. If the king were ever to visit his village, a knight would be expected to know how to welcome the king and how to feed and entertain his entourage.

Before the squire could become a full-fledged knight, which was a prerequisite to going into battle, he took part in the ceremony of knighthood. Following a bath and dressing in clean white linen clothes, the young squire was led to the village chapel to receive his sword. Following an oath of allegiance to the king, his sword was fastened around his waist and spurs were attached to his boots. At that moment, he became a full-fledged member of the nobility.

Once a knight, remaining in top condition during times of peace was the highest priority. Various games, such as jousting tournaments, dueling with dulled sword blades, and archery contests, were organized to keep each fighter's skills finely honed. But the one activity most enjoyed by all the men living in the manor house was the hunt.

The Hunt

At dawn on summer days, when the deer were at their fattest, the lord and his guests mounted their horses, gathered their hunting dogs, and headed into the lord's forests

---

Dispensing Manorial Justice

Lords of the manor heard complaints, determined innocence and guilt, and levied fines. Calvin College's online article "Extracts from the Halmote Court Rolls of the Prior and Convent of Durham, 1345–83" provides a glimpse into village justice. The following list represents some of the complaints brought against people and the fines levied by the local lord:

Billingham, 1364. It is enjoined upon all the tenants of the vill [village] that none of them grind his grain outside of the domain so long as the mill of the lord prior is able to grind, under penalty of 20s.

Coupon, 1365. From Alice of Belasis, for bad ale, and moreover because the ale which she sent to the Terrar was of no strength, as was proved in court, 2s.

Newton Bewley, 1365. From John of Baumburg for his transgression against Adam of Marton, in calling him false, perjured, and a rustic; to the loss of the same Adam of Marton 40d, penalty 13d.

Mid-Merrington, 1365. It is enjoined upon all the tenants of the vill that none of them insult the pounder [thresher] while fulfilling his duty, nor swear at him.

Newton Bewley, 1368. From Thomas, servant of the same [Adam of Marton] for drawing his knife to strike John Smith, penalty 40d, by grace 12d.

for a day of hunting, the favorite pastime for a medieval lord and the source of meat for his table. This was also an opportunity for the male members of the family to practice their military maneuvers, the principal obligation of the village nobility. Since this activity was also a social event, the ladies followed and watched at a safe distance.

The noblemen did their best to maintain forests for their own private use. They passed laws so that no peasants could hunt large game in the forests, and in this way the lords were free to hunt in the forest all of the time. The prey was usually a stag, a doe, or a wild boar. The hunt began when the huntsman, a member of the lord's staff, tracked down a deer or wild boar using his hounds. If the lord determined that the animal was large enough to pursue, the huntsman and his dogs would chase it out into a clearing where the mounted hunting party was waiting to give chase.

The fast-action chase was filled with quick, exciting equestrian maneuvers, including jumping over fallen logs, charging across streams, and crashing through thick brush. Local peasants sometimes climbed to the tops of trees to watch the hunters as they charged through the brush and woods. When the stag or wild boar was cornered, both hounds and hunters moved in for the kill.

Sometimes things did not go well for the hunters. Dangers included falling and breaking one's bones, being accidentally shot by an arrow intended for the game, or worse. The wild boar was the most dangerous of all animals because it could attack the horses with its razor-sharp tusks. "The boar slayeth a man with one stroke, as with a knife," says the unknown author of the fifteenth-century hunting treatise *The Master of Game*. "Some have seen him slit a man from knee to breast and slay him stark dead with one stroke."[10]

After the members of the hunting party had killed the stag or boar, they brought its carcass to the manor house, where it was then cut up. The butcher gathered the internal organs, placed them on a stick, and threw them to the dogs that had taken part in the chase. Following this carnage, the nobles filed into the manor house to enjoy a great feast of the freshly hunted animals.

The hunt as a form of military exercise reminded everyone that the lord and other nobles might be called upon to leave for a war either nearby or far away. When the lord left the village, mounted on his horse and in full armor, the running of the village was turned over to the lord's many administrative assistants. These were handpicked men whose jobs were to provide both general administration of the village as well as direct contact with the most important village businessmen, such as the miller, the baker, the butcher, and the blacksmith.

The Village Workers

2

Physical isolation and political independence were two of the defining characteristics of the medieval village. For this reason, each village needed to function as a self-contained entity capable of supplying all of its citizens' needs, a necessity that demanded a variety of workers skilled in many different professions and crafts. Regardless of where they worked or what jobs they performed, each member of the village had a particular role or trade that had been handed down from father to son, and each was dependent upon all the others for survival. Over many generations, a refined mix of village leaders, village officials, craftsmen, and unskilled labor evolved to serve the needs of all villagers.

The Steward

The steward was the highest-ranking village worker who was not a member of the nobility. He functioned as a lord's chief officer, overseeing lands and villagers. His principal jobs were to guard over the lord's property and animals in a reasonable and fair manner and to defend the rights of the lord in all of his dealings with the villagers. The steward reported directly to the lord but was not directly involved in the day-to-day administration of the village, especially in the case of a lord who controlled several villages.

Much of the steward's time was spent roaming the village on horseback taking general account of the work being done by peasants, being aware of any transactions taking place between villagers, inspecting and resolving all problems that might arise within the village, and having a general awareness

A page from a thirteenth-century manuscript depicts medieval trade and industry.

of village life. He was especially interested in seeing that everyone was hard at work at his or her job, whether it was farming, baking bread, grazing sheep, or milking cows. He was equally concerned with all interactions within the village to ensure that all debts and rents were paid, all customers were treated fairly, and all laws were enforced fairly.

In the absence of the lord, there was no one to oversee the steward. A few historical records report that stewards could live an honorable and honest life on their annual pay and stay out of debt, but many preferred to live more affluently. To do so, they padded their incomes by withholding some rent money from the lord as well as by overcharging some villagers and pocketing the extra money.

The Bailiff

The second-most-important assistant to the lord, but the most important in the eyes of the villagers, was the bailiff. He worked closely with the villagers as the chief law enforcement officer and the business manager responsible for overseeing the day-to-day activities of the village. In 1380 the village of Maldon, England, required each new bailiff to swear this traditional oath before assum-

The village steward was responsible for overseeing the lord's lands and accounting for work done by peasants like those pictured here.

ing office: "To well and truly govern the town and maintain its franchises [businesses]; To give equal justice to all men, without favor to any party; To supervise the sale of goods coming by water and see that all burgesses [citizens] have their share."[11]

The bailiff's day began early. First he patrolled the village by horseback, conducting a general survey of the manor's woods, meadows, fields, and pastures. He then checked to see that such things as the oxen were yoked to plows early in the morning, manure was properly spread across fields, the lord's forests were free of poachers, and sheep were grazing in the agreed-upon meadows. One historical account describing the hiring of a bailiff in Canterbury explains the bailiff's farm responsibilities: "To cause the land to be sewn, reaped, manured and cultivated, and all the wagons and ploughs and cattle together with the sheep, lambs, hogs and all other head of stock there to be managed and tended as shall seem best for our profit."[12]

As payment for all of his work, the bailiff received some money and some special privileges. According to historians Frances and Joseph Gies in their book *Life in a Medieval Village,* the bailiff of the village of Elton, England, received "twenty shillings a year plus room and board, a fur coat, fodder for his horse, and twopence to make his Christmas obligation [offering]."[13] In addition to this compensation, the bailiff and his family enjoyed the additional benefit of living in the lord's manor house and eating their meals there along with other members of the household staff.

Yet like the steward, many bailiffs lined their pockets with ill-gotten gains. Bailiffs were particularly susceptible to bribery because unscrupulous ones could choose not to notice infractions of the law. The village of Peasmarsh, England, for example, had a law preventing "the burying of stinking bodies before the arrival of the coroner."[14] In 1248, however, a body was found in a field, yet when the bailiff was summoned to investigate, according to a coroner's report, a group of men "bribed their bailiff, with forty shillings, not to call the coroner."[15]

The Reeve

Assisting the bailiff was a man called the reeve, whose responsibilities were to ensure that the farmers who owed labor services to the lord rose promptly and reported for work. The reeve supervised the formation of plow teams in the morning and made sure that the lord's livestock was properly placed in pens. He also ordered the mending of any fences that were broken, and ensured that sufficient forage, such as hay, oats, and corn, was put aside for the winter months when the cold prevented livestock from grazing in the open fields.

The reeve also kept an eye on the herdsmen and plowmen to make sure that they did not disappear from the job or rest the oxen too long. Farm life was difficult, and the lure of a fair in a neighboring village, an impromptu wrestling match, or a tavern with a new barrel of ale attracted the attention of many hard laborers eager to escape the drudgery of the lord's fields. When the reeve found a worker who had wandered away from his duties, he ordered him back to work and, if necessary, summoned the bailiff to assist him.

But of all of the reeve's numerous responsibilities, the most important to the lord was his accounting of the agricultural land at the end of the year. Accounts that have survived indicate that most of these were divided into four parts: money owed to the lord, expenses

An illustrated page from a thirteenth-century book depicts a reeve delivering collected taxes to a nobleman.

and delivery charges, inventory of grains stored in the granary, and livestock. The reeve, like most other villagers, was illiterate, yet he was still responsible for maintaining these accounts. To accomplish this feat, the reeve kept tally of everything on a stick called the tally stick. The tallies were notched with a knife in a form of shorthand that he would later read off to a scribe for formal documentation on parchment paper.

In return for his accounting of all of the lord's assets and liabilities, the reeve received no cash but was exempted from any taxes and received some of his meals at the manor house table. On occasion, some lords allowed the reeve to graze his sheep on their pasture free of charge. In other villages, the lord allowed the reeve to remove as many vegetables as he liked from the manor vegetable garden.

Yet, as was the case with all of the lord's assistants, the compensation was never sufficient. Like the steward and the bailiff, writers of the time reported that because the reeves received no direct income, they too took advantage of the villagers to fatten their wallets. As the controller of the tally stick, the reeve was in a position to add to or subtract from a true count of livestock or quantity of grain. By accepting bribes from farmers, all but the lord could profit by a fraudulent accounting of the fall harvest.

As important to the smooth functioning of the village as the officials and the farmers was the work performed by dozens of small-business owners. Although the lord did not appoint businessmen or craftsmen, they still owed the lord taxes and other levies in return for the use of buildings, water, wood, and other natural resources controlled by the lord. In every medieval village there were many types of small-business owners, but the most important were the miller, the baker, the butcher, and the blacksmith, who commonly took the names of their profession as their own last names: Miller, Baker, Butcher, and Smith.

The Miller

The miller was indispensable to the daily lives of everyone in the village. Every village had at least one miller, whose job it was to mill grain seeds into flour so that it could be used for breads, pie crusts, cereal, dinner rolls, and pastry shells for meat dishes. Grains such as wheat, corn, oats, or barley could be safely stored for long periods without damage, but the same was not true of flour. Flour could rot if it became moist or infested with worms. For this reason, villagers made trips to the mill on a weekly basis.

The miller built his mill on the lord's land. This caused him to be indebted to the lord for allowing him to build his mill on the lord's land and for using the lord's river to turn the mill's waterwheel. The cost to the miller was high: The lord took a percent of all flour milled,

called a multure, an amount that would be sufficient to meet the baking needs of his family. To pay the lord and himself, millers collected between one-sixteenth and one-twentieth of the grain brought in for milling.

The miller lived in a room above his mill so that he could begin his day early. He first inspected the waterwheel's many wood gears to make sure they were functioning properly. The waterwheel rotated his two horizontally mounted, heavy stone milling wheels that ground and pulverized the grain into baking flour. After inspecting his machinery, he pulled a lever that engaged the waterwheel; this set the top stone in motion, which crushed the grain in a tiny space between it and the stationary bottom stone.

When the villagers brought in their sacks of grain, the miller hoisted them to a chute directly above the flat millstones and dumped them in. The chute fed the grain down a tube to the center of the two stones so that the seeds tumbled out in between the two grinding surfaces. As the stones pulverized the grain, the flour spilled out onto the floor. When the milling was finished, the miller scooped the flour into bags, weighed them, subtracted his multure, and handed the rest to the customer.

The skill of a good miller was his ability to carefully adjust the space between the two stones. Each type of grain differed in size, and the miller needed to be certain that the space was small enough to thoroughly crush the small seeds—about three times the thickness of a fingernail for wheat—but not too close because the spinning granite stones might touch, creating enough friction to burn the wheat. To ensure that the stones were not touching, the miller kept his nose close to the grindstone to smell for burning wheat.

No businessman was more suspected of fraud than the miller. He performed the milling, weighing, multure, and bagging of the grain away from his waiting customers. This caused him to fall under suspicion of taking more than his fair share or of mixing old, poor-quality grains with the fresh ones brought in by the customer. So common was the latter problem that the village of Ipswich, England, passed a law stating, "Upon pain of punishment, it is forbidden that any storer of corn [grain], miller, or anyone else mix rotten corn [grain] in with good corn [grain] with the intent of selling it in Ipswich, to deceive townsfolk or outsiders."[16]

So notorious was the reputation of millers in general for taking too much multure that many jokes were told about them. Suspicion ran so high within many villages that a commonly told riddle asked the question, "What is the boldest thing in the world?" The reply was, "A miller's shirt, for it clasps a thief by the throat daily."[17]

The Baker

The baker was the second-most-needed merchant in the village. Baking bread required a hot oven that burned more wood than a peasant family could afford. To circumvent this problem, all villagers purchased their bread two or three times a week at the local bakery.

The baker's day began long before the first patrons arrived at sunrise. Starting at two A.M., the baker's first task was to chop wood. After that, he started a fire to heat his oven to the desired temperature, which took between one and two hours.

The Village Millstones

The village gristmill was the largest piece of machinery driven by waterpower in medieval Europe. Small hand-turned mills were available that were capable of grinding small quantities of grain, more commonly called grist. But to grind the volume of grain into the flour needed to supply hundreds or thousands of people, the larger water-driven wheels were required.

At the heart of the milling process were the two identical circular stones that were anywhere between four and six feet in diameter and three feet thick. The two stones were always manufactured to be precisely the same size and were made from the same type of hard stone, usually granite. The stones were set flat at the mill, one directly on top of the other, with a small space in between them. The bottom stone, called the bed stone, was permanently set and was immobile, but the top one, called the runner stone, turned at about one hundred revolutions per minute. The power to turn the two- to three-ton runner stone was provided by the waterwheel, which transmitted its power to the stone by way of a series of gears. The grinding surfaces of each stone had hundreds of small grooves, about an eight-inch deep, that radiated out from the center to the edge and channeled out the flour as the wheel spun.

The miller fed the grain seeds into a hopper above the two stones, when gradually fed the seeds down a chute in the center. As the seeds spilled into the narrow space between the spinning top stone, they were ground into flour. The flour was then carried to the outer edge in the grooves by the centrifugal force of the spinning wheel and was deposited on the floor, where it was then collected and scooped into bags.

The village baker was an important merchant. Here, a traveling baker with a portable oven delivers his goods.

While the fire warmed his oven, the baker, his wife, and sometimes an assistant gathered the needed ingredients for their breads. Most breads were made with basic ingredients that were very similar regardless of the type of breads being baked. Most breads began with flour, either wheat, rye, or barley; milk; salt; and yeast. Besides these basic ingredients, bakers occasionally added nuts and dried fruits for special holiday breads. And at least a few loaves of bread were made with beans and lentils for the poor and as feed for the lord's horses.

While the bread rose in wooden loaf containers called trenchers, the baker placed a stamp on each loaf identifying it as a loaf made in his bakery and began the process of continually monitoring the temperature of his oven. The oven was typically a large domed structure standing several feet high and in some cases up to six feet in diameter. The oven had thick walls made of a combination of stone, clay, and brick. The oven's smooth cement floor was where the baker would place his bread. The front of the oven had a very small opening for loading and unloading the oven. The small opening was also where the baker tested the temperature of the oven before beginning the day's baking. If the oven was too hot or too cold, it would ruin his day's bread. After years of experience, the baker could hold his cheek next to the small opening to determine when the time was right to remove the remaining ashes

The Baker's Mark

After a baker formed his bread dough into loaves, but before baking it, he marked each loaf. The mark, which was unique to each baker, identified the bakery of origin. The marking of bread, like that of beer barrels and many other products, became obligatory throughout Europe during the fifteenth century. The bakers were required to choose a mark the day they set up shop.

The mark was often the first letter of the baker's name or sometimes a figurative representation. The most noticeable were figures such as a baker's cap, a local flower, a crescent, a star, a cross, or a small bird. The mark was applied to each loaf by a small wooden or lead die, which was registered on a parchment at the nearest large city. It was severely forbidden for master bakers to change the mark without permission.

The seal also served to identify any baker who might cheat his customers by selling loaves of bread that were short of weight, unwholesome, mixed with sawdust, or half-baked. But if a man consistently made good bread, his seal would naturally come to be associated with his high standard. To sell bread without a mark, therefore, exposed the baker at once to the suspicion of trying to pass off a bad product. Worse than not marking one's own loaves, however, was being caught using another man's mark. This meant that the real owner of the seal was in danger of being punished for another's defects or that one baker was trading on another's reputation.

of the burning wood to prevent the temperature from becoming too hot. When the oven reached the desired temperature, the baker removed the risen loaves from the trenchers and slid them into the oven with long-handled wooden paddles. The thick walls retained the heat for several hours, allowing the baker to complete all of his baking without having to reheat his oven. In the course of baking, the baker moved bread from place to place within the oven to ensure even baking. During this process, bakers often singed their knees, giving them the name "crusty knees" by the locals.

Drawings from the Middle Ages show bakers clamped in the village stocks—a wood apparatus, usually situated in a public square, that clamped around a person's neck and hands to prevent him or her from fleeing—with a loaf of bread hanging around their necks. This sort of public humiliation was meted out whenever villagers caught their baker cheating by selling underweight bread, half-baked loafs, or using inferior ingredients, which might include sawdust.

The Butcher

The butcher was never as significant in the medieval village as the miller or the baker because many villagers could not afford butchered meat. Nonetheless, each village had several butchers, whose trademark was the wave of a three- or four-fingered hand; missing fingers was a common liability of the profession. Slaughtering and carving up large animals such as cows, horses, pigs, goats, and sheep with sharp knives was the job of the butcher, who left the butchering of smaller commonly eaten animals like rabbits, fowl, fish, and squirrels to each family.

The butcher served the needs of those desiring fresh meat who could afford it. The butchers' quarters in each village were located near rivers and streams, far from village centers. This isolation was because of the amount of blood that flowed from slaughtering animals and the need to dispose of all nonedible viscera by washing it into rivers. In 1439, in the village of Lynn, England, a law was passed aimed at eliminating the stench of blood in the streets: "Henceforth the entrails of all animals slaughtered in the southern part of town are to be carted to Le Balle and there cast [into the river] at the low-tide mark at the time of half-ebb."[18]

Shoppers who came to the butchers' quarters witnessed the slaughter. An animal was held still by ropes looped over a beam and tightly wrapped around both back legs as a butcher slit the throat of the animal. Helpers immediately hoisted the legs into the air while another slid an iron pot under the neck to catch the blood that would become the main ingredient for blood pudding and blood sausage.

The butcher then laid the animal on a bench to carve it up. Price was determined by the size of the cut of meat, and most purchases were for large amounts—hind sections, quarter sections, half a cow, rib cages, the entire skull—most of which would be taken home and dried, smoked, or salted for later consumption. Butchers wore an iron-mesh corset under their aprons, called a belly belt. It deflected the sharp knives that sometimes

A pane of stained glass shows a medieval butcher at work in his quarters.

were drawn so forcefully through an animal's flesh that they accidentally cut all the way through and grazed the butchers' own stomachs.

The major complaint that villagers had with butchers was the freshness of meat. Although most customers preferred to witness an animal being slaughtered to guarantee its freshness, they could not always be present. To protect customers, most villages passed laws prohibiting the sale of old meat. The major complaint that farmers had with butchers, however, was their inclination to steal, kill, and butcher livestock and then bring the carved pieces to the village market for sale. To put an end to this illegal practice, many villages, like Ipswich, passed ordinances like this one:

Much evil handiwork has often been done in the countryside through theft of livestock, and the carcasses have been sold in the village by butchers, thus giving the village a bad reputation in the countryside. Therefore it is ordained that no butcher henceforth bring into the village to sell any carcasses of beef, veal, or mutton, unless he bring the skins and hides with the carcasses, so that any man seeking his stolen animals might be able to identify them through the skins and hides.[19]

The Blacksmith

Not as valued as the mill, bakery, or butcher shop, the village smithy was nonetheless an

This medieval painting shows a gathering of peasants and tradesmen, including a blacksmith with a pair of iron tongs (foreground).

important and busy shop. It also happened to be one of the few where patrons did not feel cheated. The job of the village blacksmith, who worked in the smithy, was to fabricate functional objects made of iron. The blacksmith was called on to make many products for the villagers' farms, including iron hitches for wagons and plows, iron plowshares, and iron wagon wheels. For the household, he made common objects such as door locks, hinges, and knobs.

In order to shape the iron, a blacksmith heated it red or white hot to soften it. This process required four trademark pieces of equipment: the forge, which was an iron furnace filled with charcoal for heating iron; the bellows, for increasing the temperature of the furnace by injecting blasts of air; a sledgehammer for pounding the hot iron into shape; and an anvil, which was a heavy iron platform on which the iron was pounded. Typically the piece of iron to be shaped was placed directly into the hot charcoal. The blacksmith then pumped the bellows with his leg, increasing the temperature dramatically. With his tongs he turned the iron over until its color indicated it was ready to be removed and worked on the anvil.

Thousands of hours of pounding iron with his hammer often embedded tiny iron chips in the back of the blacksmith's hand that held the work. When visitors to a village wanted to know how much experience a blacksmith had, they would ask him to "show his metal." The blacksmith understood that this meant to show them the back of his hand so they could see the amount of embedded iron as an indication of his years of experience.

All of the blacksmith's work was traded to his customers for payment in kind. However, this sometimes created interesting negotiations. For example, if a farmer asked for a plow hitch, to one farmer it might be worth four chickens; to another one, a small pig; and yet to still a third, a sack of wheat. The blacksmith was always motivated by what he needed at the time and the importance of not alienating any of his customers by asking for too much. Unlike the miller and the baker, the village blacksmith was not the only one of his profession in the village—another person might challenge him by opening a second shop.

Working in the village shops or as an assistant to the lord was hard work, but at least it was consistent. The same could not be said for the majority of peasant workmen who rose early each day to work in the fields without the certainty of producing a good crop at the end of the year.

A Calendar of Toil

Toil was the ruling fact of life in all medieval villages. No group understood that better than farmers, who usually comprised between 70 and 80 percent of the population. They were the backbone of every village's economy. They worked the entire year. By the time the first light of day crossed the horizon, oxen were yoked and plows were hitched as a cavalcade of farmers and their helpers set out down dirt roads to their fields. They would toil up one row and down the next until the setting sun freed them to return to their cottages for the night.

The economy of each village revolved around its agriculture. A variety of grains were the primary cash crops for most villagers, along with livestock, sheep that were shorn for their wool, chickens, and dairy cows that provided milk, cream, butter, and cheese. The hopes for good crops in the late summer began with plowing the fields in early spring to prepare them for planting.

Plowing Fields

The agricultural cycle in a medieval village began in the spring, when April showers softened the earth and when farmers prepared the land for planting. This was the most labor-intensive form of work in the village. Very poor farmers were forced to use the scratch plow, so named because it did little more than scratch a shallow furrow across the field. Since the plowshare, the cutting point of a plow, was only three to four inches in diameter and penetrated not more than one foot, the farmer and his ox or horse had to plow in a north-south direction and then east-west to create a crosshatched effect on the field.

Fortunately for the village farmers with a little extra money, a more efficient plow could be purchased with two additional features. This better plow had a metal cutting blade mounted in front of the plowshare that made the first cut to break up the sod. Behind the metal blade was the moldboard, a wooden device attached to the plow just behind the plowshare. It rolled the plowed earth over. These two inventions revolutionized plowing because the new plowshare could cut deeper into the soil, and with the moldboard it was not necessary to crosshatch the field.

However, with this more efficient plow came the need for more horses or oxen. More efficient plows requiring more draft animals meant that several farmers shared their animals. Common sense of the time, expressed by Walter of Henley, a thirteenth-century writer on agriculture, recommended the use of oxen over horses because horses required a stall during the winter, costing "one halfpenny a week for oats—and at least twelve pennyworth of grass in the summer, and a penny a week in shoeing."[20] Besides, the oxen could be eaten when they got old.

As a team moved across a field, one farmer walked behind the plow, controlling its position and the depth of the plowshare.

A medieval farmer uses a scratch plow to plant his fields in this thirteenth-century painting.

A second person walked next to the animals with a whip to keep them pulling at a steady pace and in a straight line. Keeping them moving was crucial because regaining momentum after a stop was extremely difficult. Following along behind the plow was a third person, whose job it was to break up any clods of dirt or any heavy clay chunks rolled over by the moldboard. Sketches drawn of the plowmen during this time sometimes depict workers beating the large clay clods with mallets and hammers; other sketches depict both men and women stomping on the clods with their bare feet.

The plowing task that required the greatest skill was turning a large team of animals at the end of each furrow and then heading back in the opposite direction. The turn had to be a quick U-turn, and it had to be precise to avoid plowing through someone else's furrows or over furrows already plowed. Accomplishing this U-turn correctly required a great deal of coordination and experience on the part of the farmer. When the person controlling the team swung them around, the man controlling the plow tipped it over onto its side and allowed it to slide along on the surface of the soil. He then quickly got it upright and forced

The Pastoureaux Revolts

The misery of the rural poor in the wake of mounting taxes occasionally triggered a revolt, called a Pastoureaux, against the village lord. In 1250 a peasant by the name of Pastoureaux began a mass peasant uprising in France against the lords of many villages. The village peasants understood very clearly that they lived lives oppressed by the nobility and that they were forever struggling against the lord's effort to squeeze more and more taxes, goods, and services out of them.

The disparity of wealth and the oppression of the peasant by the landowner troubled the conscience of many people during the Middle Ages. Historian Barbara Tuchman, in her book *A Distant Mirror: The Calamitous Fourteenth Century*, cites the thirteenth-century author Jacques de Vitry as delivering a sermon and calling out, "Ye nobles are like raving wolves. Therefore shall ye howl in hell . . . who despoil your subjects and live on the blood and sweat of the poor." What ever the poor manage to save in one year, de Vitry continued, "The knight and noble devour in an hour."

As waves of Pastoureaux occasionally rolled across the European countryside, peasants refused to plow the lords' fields, thresh his grain, or grind their flour at his mill. Despite fines, this sometimes went on for years and sometimes erupted into violence and murder. De Vitry warned the nobility, "If they can aid us, they can also do us harm. You know that many peasants have killed their masters or have burned their houses."

The largest Pastoureaux ever, the Great Peasant Revolt, occurred in England in 1381, and following years of bloodshed and eventual riots by tens of thousands of peasants in London, King Richard II was forced to negotiate with the peasant leaders. Although the king agreed to a long list of peasants' rights, he shortly thereafter killed the leaders and brutally crushed the rebellion.

---

the plowshare back into the soil the instant that the team had completed its turn.

Sowing

While the spring soil was still soft and moist from plowing, farmers began sowing the fields. They used seeds left over from the previous year's harvest. Considered the easiest of all farming tasks, sowing had to be done immediately to take advantage of the condition of the field; waiting too long might jeopardize the germination of the seeds. Seeds needed the soft moist soil to germinate and for their roots to take hold.

Once all large clods of dirt had been broken into smaller pieces, the farmer and his wife cast seeds by hand in broad sweeps as they walked down the furrows. This method of sowing, called broadcasting, guaranteed that every square inch of soil would produce several young shoots within two to three weeks. The four grains most widely planted were wheat, barley, rye, and oats. Of these, wheat was most valued because it had the gluten content necessary to make good bread.

On occasion, two or three varieties of grain were sown together by the broadcast method in a mixture known as dredge. Peas and beans were painstakingly dibbled, the seeds being placed in a series of small holes made by poking a stick known as a dibbler or dibbling stick into the ground. Choosing the right amount of seed to sow was a delicate matter that depended on soil quality and, to some extent, local custom. If there were too few seeds, weeds would choke the growing crops; if there were too many, the crops would choke themselves. Many farmers recommended that barley should be sown at four bushels to the acre and oats, peas, and beans at three bushels to the acre.

As the seeds were planted, crows, blackbirds, wrens, and pigeons swooped down to feed. Young boys skilled in the use of the slingshot followed behind the planters to kill these predatory birds. Not only did the boys provide the farmers a valuable service of protecting the newly planted seeds, but they also carried home many fine fowl dinners for their families. Boys enjoyed this form of hunting, but they knew not to kill any doves because they were prized game birds of the nobility; killing one brought a heavy penalty. Because they were protected, doves caused considerable damage to crops, which made them a hated symbol of the lord's power.

The seeds were quickly covered by soil to protect them from birds and the drying sun. This was called harrowing. The simplest, cheapest, and most ineffective harrows were bundles of brushwood dragged behind a horse —sometimes even tied to its tail. More sturdy

A peasant farmer's wife often joined her husband in the labor of planting and harvesting.

A Calendar of Toil 39

harrows consisted of wooden or iron pegs fixed into a wooden frame. These rakes were pulled over the seeds to cover them with earth. When the fields were sown and covered, children made scarecrows to set in the fields to help scare away the crows and other birds.

Harvesting Crops

Knowing when to harvest was just as important as knowing how to harvest. In late summer, around mid-August or early September, farmers walked down their grain fields testing their crops to determine whether they were ready to be harvested. Many farmers had a specific way of testing their crops. For example, a farmer would wade into his field, break the heads off one or two grain stalks, grind the heads into the palm of his hand, blow away the chaff, and then taste the seeds. Nibbling away at them with his front teeth, he tested for moisture content. If his teeth eased into the moist, spongy seeds, the heads were not yet ready to be harvested because wet seeds would rot. When his teeth met resistance and then suddenly snapped through the seeds, nearly chipping his teeth, the hard seeds were dry and ready to be harvested.

At harvest time, the race was on. All villagers joined in the harvest—the old and young, men and women, vagabonds and criminals—time was of the essence. Failure to bring the crops in as quickly as possible jeopardized the entire year's work. Without notice, a hailstorm might destroy an entire field; likewise, a sudden rainstorm might knock down the crop, making harvesting far more difficult. Sometimes locusts might devour the field right before the farmer's eyes, or an invading army might steal it for food.

The grain stalks were cut by an army of village workers sprinkled across the field.

They used two simple tools: a wooden stick with a curved end, called a hook; and a small, curved, sharp, iron scythe, also called a sickle. Holding the hook in one hand and the sickle in the other, each laborer reached out and hooked a bundle of twenty to thirty grain shafts, gathered them close together in the neck of the hook, and then with the sickle in the other hand, cut the bundle and dropped it to the ground. A worker then moved on and continued this rhythmic process all day long.

Following closely behind the harvesters were the binders. Their first job was to pick up the cut grain lying on the ground and gather it into bundles, called shocks or sheaves. Failure to get the grain off the ground might mean having it trampled or soaked in a sudden rainstorm. These sheaves usually measured about the diameter of a man's outstretched arms—and contained about four to five hundred stalks—with the grain heads at one end and the straw stalks at the other. The binders then wrapped string around the bundle; when they had three bundles, they stood them up in the field with the grain heads at the top, leaning toward the center to form a triangle.

Threshing the Grain

Following the binding, young boys and girls were sent through the fields to gather and carry the bundles on their backs to a cart. After the bundles were gathered, they were transported to a threshing floor in the center of a barn. Threshing was the process of separating the grain seeds from the chaff and stems. This was dirty, dusty, and hard work.

The sheaves were placed on the barn floor or some other flat surface where doors at either end could be opened to provide a breeze to cool the workers and to clear the

The Wisdom of Walter of Henley

A writer on farming topics, Walter of Henley wrote one of the earliest treatises on farming, called *Treatise on Husbandry,* in about 1270. It is his only known work on husbandry, and it provides simple villagers with practical knowledge and advice on farming. The following are some excerpts from his treatise:

Survey your lands and tenements by your sworn men:

Some men will tell you that a plough cannot work eight score [160] or nine score [180] acres yearly, but I will show you that it can. You know well that a furlong [220 yards] ought to be forty perches long and four wide, and the king's perch is sixteen feet and a half; then an acre is sixty-six feet in width [an acre is one furlong (40 perches, or 220 yards) long and four perches (22 yards) wide]. Now in ploughing go thirty-six times round to make the ridge narrower, and when the acre is ploughed then you have made seventy-two furlongs, which are six leagues, for be it known that twelve furlongs are a league [1.5 miles]. And the horse or ox must be very poor that cannot from the morning go easily in pace three leagues in length from his starting place and return by three o'clock.

How you must keep your oxen:

And if the ox is to be in a condition to do his work, then it is necessary that he should have at least three sheaves and a half of oats in the week, price one penny, and ten sheaves of oats should yield a bushel of oats in measure; and in summer twelve pennyworth of grass: the sum three shillings, one penny, without fodder or chaff. And when the horse is old and worn out then there is nothing but the skin; and when the ox is old, with ten pennyworth of grass he shall be fit for the larder, or will sell for as much as he cost.

To sow your lands:

Sow your lands in time, so that the ground may be settled and the corn rooted before great cold. If by chance it happens that a heavy rain comes or falls on the earth within eight days of the sowing, and then a sharp frost should come and last two or three days, if the earth is full of holes the frost will penetrate through the earth as deep as the water entered, and so the corn [grain], which has sprouted and is very tender, will perish.

---

air of dust and chaff. The sheaves of grain were laid on the floor against a low wall of wood called a threshold, which held the threshed grain in place. Threshers used "hand flails"—tools made of bound strips of leather—to beat the heads of grain to separate the grains from the stems and chaff. The grain was then scooped up, poured into sacks, and stored for the next year's planting and for milling into flour.

The last step in the threshing process involved the winnowing, or gleaning, process.

This separated the remaining grain still mixed with the chaff, stems, and barn dirt. With a decent gust of wind blowing through the barn, threshers picked up the remaining chaff and grain with shovels, tossed it into the air, and as the lighter chaff blew out the door, the heavier grain seeds fell to the ground. These last seeds were then added to the grain sacks.

Once the fields had been cleared, the desperately poor, the old, and the infirm of the village were allowed to enter the fields to pick through the dirt and stems to scrape

A painting depicts a peasant using a "hand flail" to thresh a bundle of wheat.

together any seeds that had been left behind by the workers who had shocked the grain. This was the only time farmers would allow strangers to enter their fields.

Haying

As the summer days grew warmer and longer, the workload grew heavier. The hot summer was the haying season. The best land for haying was always the "bottom land," meaning the land with the lowest acreage, which was also the wettest. If farmers were lucky and the spring and summer brought both rain and hot sun, they might be able to cut two crops of hay. The hay was a food source for their livestock during the winter, when the grasses of the meadows withered beneath a blanket of snow.

Haying took place when the grass was about twelve to eighteen inches tall. Generally an entire crew of farmers, as well as any young helpers they could recruit, was pulled together to cut, rake, gather, and cart the hay of an entire field. The first workers to enter the meadow, once the morning sun had dried the evening's dew, were the mowers. They moved through the tall grass with a methodical, slow swinging of their scythe, a sharp four-foot-long blade with a slight curve attached to a two-handed handle. Always swinging from right to left, they moved down the field in a long well-coordinated line slightly overlapping the cutter standing next to them so no grass would be missed.

Although the summer days were hot, the work crews, sometimes both men and women, arrived in the morning fully dressed but barefoot. By midmorning, however, the men had removed their jackets, rolled up their sleeves, and set aside their hoods. The women also removed their outer coats and shawls. By midafternoon, when the temperature was soaring, the men stripped to the waist, and the women shortened their dresses by tying them off to the side well above their knees or tucked the hem into the belt to keep it out of the way.

As soon as an acre or so of hay lay on the field, rakers, usually adolescent girls and boys, raked the hay into small mounds using wooden rakes with wooden pegs for teeth. The mounds were then easily picked up and carried by men using wooden pronged pitchforks. Each mound was carried to a horse-drawn cart and was piled high in a stack until no more could be loaded. The cart was then driven to a barn, where the hay was unloaded and stored for winter use. The key to preserving the hay and having it retain its nutrient value for later feeding to the village livestock was to keep it dry.

On occasion, when all of the barns were full and overflowing, excess hay was stacked in the fields like giant loaves of bread. Stacks were rectangular, about eight to ten feet high, with a round dome on top to shed winter rains. When properly stacked to repel water, the outer hay turned brown and looked like dry tinder; however, a foot beneath the

"The Haymaker's Song"

On occasion, stories about the work and lives of village farmers were told in songs. "The Haymaker's Song," found on the Poet's Corner website, is one such example that was written at the end of the Middle Ages and was sung at summer festivals during the hay season. It tells about the work of haymakers and their leisure time:

In the merry month of June,
In the prime time of the year;
Down in yonder meadows
There runs a river clear:
And many a little fish
Doth in that river play;
And many a lad, and many a lass,
Go abroad a-making hay.

In come the jolly mowers,
To mow the meadows down;
With budget and with bottle
Of ale, both stout and brown,
Allabouringng, [a German surname]
    men of courage bold
Come here their strength to try;
They sweat and blow, and cut and mow,
For the grass cuts very dry.

And when that bright day faded,
And the sun was going down,
There was a merry piper
Approached from the town:
He pulled out his pipe and tabor,
So sweetly he did play,
Which made all lay down their rakes,
And leave off making hay.

Then joining in a dance,
They jig it o'er the green;
Though tired with their labour,
No one less was seen.
But sporting like some fairies,
Their dance they did pursue,
In leading up, and casting off,
Till morning was in view.

And when that bright daylight,
The morning it was come,
They lay down and rested
Till the rising of the sun:
Till the rising of the sun,
When the merry larks do sing,
And each lad did rise and take
    his lass,
And away to hay-making.

surface, the hay was still nutritional and edible by the livestock.

Sheep Shearing and Slaughtering

In July shepherds herded the sheep that had been grazing on the common land into the barns to be shorn for their wool. There were many more sheep than people in most European countries in the Middle Ages, and wool was the most commonly used material for clothing.

Shearing was performed by shepherds using straight shears similar to very large scissors. The village blacksmith custom-made these shears from the hardest iron possible so they would have a very sharp cutting edge. During shearing season, the blacksmith was kept busy making and continually sharpening the shears.

A shepherd would secure a sheep between his legs and hold the sheep's head with one hand while shearing with the other. Boys new to shearing struggled to hold the animals still while cutting hundreds of clumps of wool over a period of the entire day. Their efforts were little improvement over the more primitive technique of running the sheep through thick hedges of holly or other thistles, which tore the wool from the sheep as they ran through. The more experienced men, however, were able to shear a sheep in one hour and produce one unbroken clump of wool.

By October, each sheep owner had to decide the number of animals he could afford to feed over the coming four cold months of winter. If the hay and corn harvest had been good, he might keep most of the sheep, but in times of drought, most of the animals would be slaughtered and eaten. For this reason, October was known in the medieval village as "blood month." During a slaughter, two people would hold down a sheep while a third slit its neck with a knife and let the blood flow into a metal container to be used as an ingredient for a variety of foods.

Preservation of the meat, a process performed by each household, involved either salting the meat, drying it, or smoking it. Salting required sprinkling one pound of salt over every four pounds of flesh, and the time needed for the salting process was one day per two hundred pounds of meat. Drying meat merely required racks to hold it. It took one man one day to load four hundred pounds of mutton onto the racks. The drying process took about two weeks.

Smoking required smokehouses and wood to dry and flavor the meat. Preparing the smokehouses took one day for four hundred pounds of lamb, and the smoking process took an additional three to four days depending on the wood, temperature, and desired taste. The meat was hung on racks in the smokehouse, and a low fire was started in a stone-lined pit. As the smoke filled the smokehouse, the meat was both dried and infused with a pleasant-tasting smoke flavor. The flavor was determined by different types of bark added to the fire. Because smoking the meat was the most complicated process, requiring a specially constructed house, several families shared a single smokehouse.

Late Winter Calving

Not all animals succumbed to the October slaughter. Each farmer wealthy enough to afford livestock always kept the best ones for breeding. To supplement their crop incomes, farmers awaited the arrival of winter for their newborn calves and lambs.

Winter calving was not left to chance. Winter was the time farmers wanted their

Peasants shear their sheep in the spring in this painting dated 1457.

cows to calve because they were too busy during the rest of the year tending to their fields. They knew that the gestation period for calves was ten months, so they controlled mating with bulls to occur in March or April to guarantee late winter calves.

Calving was also a risky process, and many calves died because the farmer was not available to assist the cow. Both the farmer and his wife took turns checking on their pregnant cows to be sure that one or both of them would be there to assist when the time came. And when it did, many complications occurred that required someone to reach well inside the cow to tug on the calf. Both the farmer and his wife worked to free the calf

before it suffocated, or if the calf came out backward, they kept the hooves together so the mother would not be injured internally.

Owning cattle was a sign of wealth during the Middle Ages and a farmer was lucky if he had one calf born each year. The death of a calf, combined with a poor harvest, could push a family into financial failure and cause them to lose their land. Fears of such realities plagued village farmers, whose lives could be difficult and bleak even in the best of times. The symbol most reflective of this hard rural life was where farming families lived. Scattered through the village, the family cottage was a sanctuary, a place for family unity, and, like the fields, a place of hard work.

Family Life in the Cottage

Many medieval families lived in poverty. The peasant farmer, in particular, worked long days and had little to show for all that work. The fourteenth-century English poet William Langland once described the peasant farmer as "a poor man, badly dressed, dead tired from work, shivering in a hovel, who lived life in the most extreme misery."[21]

The typical village family's cottage was a reflection of their poverty. Most cottages had two or three rooms: one for cooking and eating, one where the entire family slept, and perhaps a third that served as a storeroom and barn. Sometimes animals slept in this room during the winter. Although their body heat was appreciated by the family, the animals left their odor. To help mask the offen-

A medieval artist depicts a contemporary village household scene.

sive smell, packed-dirt floors were covered with straw and occasionally sprinkled with an ordinary spice to sweeten the air.

Regardless of such difficult and sometimes disheartening circumstances, all members of these hardy families learned to live together, to find occasional enjoyment in life, and to grow as families. They succeeded with very little by working hard and practicing thrift, and by making almost everything they needed.

Providing Water for the Cottage

Clean water was the most important aspect of cottage life. Its presence was a necessity for food, personal hygiene, and basic sanitation. Most villages had two options for their water supply: the local water well or the nearest stream. In either case, it was a laborious and time-consuming task that wives and children had to perform two or three times a week.

All families preferred to collect their water from the local village well for the simple reason that the water would be cleaner than water drawn from a stream. Drawing water from wells, however, was a slow process, and waiting in line was common. Water could only be drawn one bucket at a time, and the elderly along with the young struggled to pull up the weight of a full bucket. Long lines became an aggravation when one person brought a large barrel that held several bucketfuls of well water. Sometimes the stream made more sense when people were in a hurry. In either case, water was transported in wooden barrels; in "waterskins," which were waterproof leather bags; and sometimes in goatskins that had been cleaned, turned inside out, and tightly stitched to create a watertight, pliable container.

Once the water arrived home from the stream, it was dumped into a large container or into a pit dug alongside the cottage to settle. Stream water was murky because of mud and other sediment carried along with the water's flow. By allowing the water to sit in a pit or large wooden container, the heavier particles settled to the bottom, allowing the cleaner water to be skimmed off the upper layer. The highest priority for clean water was for cooking.

Meals

Villagers ate whatever food was locally grown. Most villagers were farmers rather than herdsmen, so most of their food derived from the grains of their fields and vegetables from their gardens, called crofts. Standard dinners consisted of bread, pottage, and ale —all of which were made from grains of one sort or another—with occasional additions of vegetables such as spinach, turnips, cabbage, and squash, little meat, and a few dairy products.

The major food item was bread. Families ate breads made from beans, barley, and rye baked into dark, heavy loaves. Barley bread, in particular, was synonymous with bread for the poor, but the more expensive wheat bread was the staple for the nobility. The barley bread purchased from the baker was a coarse, dark loaf weighing four pounds or more. It was regularly kept in the cottage for up to three days at a time. On the third day, these loaves became so stale that tearing and ripping at them with bare teeth risked the loss of a tooth. When bread became that hard, it was dunked into a pot of broth or soup to soften and flavor it.

After the bread, pottage, also called porridge, was the staple food. Pottage was a thick soup preferred by some to bread because it did not need to be milled and it therefore

Cottage Possessions

Possessions found inside of a village cottage were often a reflection of the peasant owner's wealth. As was the case with all things in village life, those who managed to make a little more money or produce a little more grain or wool were able to acquire more elaborate furnishings while the very poor had very little.

The very poor, perhaps 15 to 20 percent of the villagers, lived in cottages that were as miserable as their bland diets. This group would be fortunate to have a one-room thatched-roof cottage with one door and no windows in which all family members slept on piles of straw without a bed frame. Lacking any furniture, not even a table or a cupboard, all possessions were oriented toward cooking: mixing bowls, an iron cooking pot, and ceramic mixing bowls.

The middle-income peasants, perhaps 60 to 70 percent of the peasant population,

owned a two-room thatched-roof cottage with two doors and one window. This family typically owned one bed for the entire family; a folding table and benches for meals; a complete collection of iron, wood, and ceramic cooking utensils; baskets, wooden buckets; and a washtub.

The affluent few, never more than 10 percent, had the luxury of a three-room cottage with a wooden frame roof, two doors, and several windows. Parents and children slept on separate feather beds with linen sheets. They usually owned two or three permanent tables, metal cooking bowls made of pewter and copper, several iron skillets, and two cooking pots. These cottages might be the only ones to have a lamp for evening light and might even have towels and napkins that were brought out for special occasions. For the very fortunate, a wooden cupboard held all cooking and eating bowls and utensils.

escaped the multure of the miller. The basis of pottage was a mixture of boiled grains, which provided protein and bulk, blended with vegetables for their vitamins, including onions, cabbage, potatoes, turnips, peas, garlic, leeks, spinach, and parsley. Occasionally these vegetables were cooked alone and became known as "potherbs"; they were often reheated day after day, as is indicated in many traditional children's rhymes of the time, such as this one: "Pease porridge hot, pease porridge cold, Pease porridge in the pot, nine days old."

Besides basic heavy breads and pottage, the peasant diet occasionally included a few delicacies provided by their livestock and gardens. Dairy products from their own goats and cows provided milk and cream, but the

butter they produced was sold to the lady of the manor house or to wealthier villagers or was traded for slices of cheese for the holidays. Chunks of pork and mutton, strung up from interior beams to keep them away from rats and dogs, occasionally flavored meals. If neighbors came to visit, an inferior slab of bacon was offered so the men could chew the fat. Often the true taste of their meat, which had to be dried, smoked, or salted to preserve it, was improved by the addition of common spices such as pepper, clove, and cinnamon, as well as by herbs from their gardens.

The fifteenth-century English poet John Glower described the typical meal in a village household as heavy on bread and water. Glower wrote, "Laborers of olden times were not wont to eat wheaten bread; their bread was of common grain or of barley and beans, and their drink was of the spring [water]. Then cheese and milk were a feast to them; rarely had they any other feast than this."[22]

Mealtime

Meals in the cottages were eaten as a necessity for sustaining life, not as entertainment. Generally two meals were eaten: breakfast and dinner. Dinnertime in the cottages did not have the same festive tone found at the elegantly set tables of the nobility, where exotic meats, cheeses, and desserts were common fare.

The cooking of all meals was the responsibility of the women and children. A large part of each day was spent making preparations for meals, especially the evening meal.

One of the most time-consuming chores was sending someone to the woods to collect fallen tree limbs and branches, hauling them home, and chopping them for firewood. Fresh vegetables had to be gathered from the croft and chopped, once a week a sack of grain needed to be hauled to the mill for milling into flour, and bread needed to be purchased or bartered from the local baker. Cleaning the cooking utensils, the least favorite chore, meant hauling everything outside and down to the nearest stream for washing. Families used sand as an abrasive to scour baked-on foods.

Dinner was served on a table that was flanked by benches for seating; chairs were a rare commodity in all but the cottages of the wealthiest villagers. Food was served on trenchers. Typically the pottage that was thick with vegetables and grains was ladled

This thirteenth-century painting shows a medieval meal prepared and served by the women and children of the household.

Part of the mealtime experience in the cottage was determined by the need to conserve fuel for cooking food. Wood was an expensive commodity because it could only be gathered from the lord's forest, and even then only fallen or dead branches could be taken. Peasants paid to gather the branches "by hook or by crook," meaning by using long wooden poles with a hook or a crook at one end to reach up and pull down dead branches.

This dearth led most poor families to perform all of their cooking over a single fire using one large cast-iron cooking pot. Many drawings of the interiors of medieval cottages depict an open fire, above which hung a large iron pot suspended by chains from the roof beam.

Typically the pot was first filled with the grains, beans, and water needed for the pottage. Small clay-covered containers, which were filled with vegetables wrapped in cloth, were then placed on the bottom of the pot. Any available meat was either chopped into very small pieces or shaped into meatballs and added to the pottage. Lastly, any starch foods, such as potatoes, parsnips, or turnips, were added for the final simmering. Using this cooking technique, the entire meal could be prepared using a small amount of wood to heat everything.

One-pot cooking also had the advantages of cooking enough food to last many days and of adding new food to the old. Peasant women savored the tradition of finding fresh foods to toss into the pot for the next day's meal. This mingling of fresh food with two- or three-day-old food fostered unusual combinations of foods. These concoctions were often named after the people who ate them, such as shepherd's pie, which combined low-quality meat with potatoes, peas, carrots, beans, potatoes, and other local vegetables. Peasant sausage pie was similar to shepherd's pie, except it contained pieces of blood sausage instead of beef. Regardless of the contents, the one-pot meal might last for a week or more before the pot was washed and a new series of meals begun.

directly on to the trencher and was eaten with a knife and sometimes a spoon. Thin pottage was sipped directly from a wooden bowl that was shared by two family members. Following dinner, the table was disassembled and stored out of the way.

Even these simple foods were a luxury in times of famine. When crops failed and animals starved, all classes of society suffered. People resorted to killing and eating their draft animals and consuming their seed grain, which meant they would have nothing to plant in the spring. Dogs, cats, and even rats disappeared from the streets. Grandparents living in the cottages often voluntarily stopped eating so younger members of the family could survive, and there were even occasional rumors of cannibalism in some villages.

Personal Hygiene

Whether working in the fields all day or tending children in the dirt-floor cottage, village people were subjected to a constant on-slaught of filth. Medieval artists occasionally depicted people bathing in local streams or ponds, but most villagers did so in their homes, especially during the colder months.

Bathing inside cottages was done in a number of different ways depending on the day of the week and on the person. Men on their way out to the fields, for example, washed only after being fully dressed—and they washed only the parts of their bodies that were visible: their face and their hands. One old document cited by historian Geneviève D'Haucort in her book *Life in the Middle Ages* made this recommendation to workmen: "In the morning when you get up, first put on your vest, then your breeches [pants], put on your waistcoat, your hood, fasten your stockings, your shoes, then put on your other clothes and tie your belt, and wash your hands, your fingers, your fingernails and your face."[23]

This habit stemmed from the fact that several people shared the same room and there were not enough places or enough water for everyone to wash properly. This does not mean that people were disinterested in more thorough bathing. Doing so, however, was a major undertaking, which required carrying enough water from a nearby stream to fill a small wooden tub, heating some or most of the water in an iron cauldron over an open fire, dumping the heated water into the tub, bathing quickly, and then disposing of the water. Considering the labor and time required for a thorough bath, it is not surprising that few people bathed more than once a week and most even less. In medieval times, the man of the house had the privilege of the first bath, followed by all of the grown sons, the women, the children, and last of all the babies. Occasionally the water became so filthy that a baby was actually thrown out with the bath water.

Dental hygiene was occasionally practiced, but only at the dinner table. For most peasants, picking at one's teeth with toothpicks was all the attention their teeth received. This practice was so commonplace that various table manner guides criticize those who did so in public places. Not only did people use toothpicks to clean their teeth at the dinner table, but one manners guide written during the sixteenth century by Giovanni della Casa, called the *Galateo*, went so far as to warn, "Avoid rubbing your teeth with your napkin or, worse still, with your fingers. . . . Let not persons eating, clean their teeth with their knife."[24]

Clothes, especially delicate clothing worn next to the skin, also required cleaning from time to time. To do this work, women headed to the nearest stream. Women made their own laundry detergent, called lye, which was made by combining ashes, lard, and water. They then soaked the clothes in the lye, beat and scrubbed them on rough pieces of hard oak or a large stone, rinsed them in the stream, and hung them out to dry in the sun. Outer garments were never laundered.

Making the Family Clothing

Peasant women, in addition to attending to the cooking, cleaning, washing, gardening, and care of the animals and children, had the responsibility of making all of the family's clothes. Peasant clothing was designed and sewn for hard outdoor work that necessitated outer garments made of rough wool. Using wool from their own sheep, village women would spin and weave the fabric, dye it the desired color, and then finally spend many hours sewing the garment.

Women first took wool to a nearby stream, where they thoroughly washed it. This process was time consuming because it

A peasant girl sits in a pastoral setting with her lamb making clothing from sheered wool.

required multiple washings while stomping on the wool to remove the natural oils. Returning to the village, the wool was hung out to dry and then spun into heavy thread using a foot-driven spinning wheel. The thread for all outer clothing was intentionally spun into course threads because it had to be strong enough to resist rough handling of livestock. Following the actual weaving of the cloth, the finished product was immersed in the dye, allowed to dry, and thoroughly washed. In the case of most outer garments, this would be the last washing ever.

The lighter clothes worn against the skin were also made of wool but with thread more finely spun. Peasant men wore woolen hose called *chausses,* which could be rolled down to allow for more freedom of movement when working. A hip-length tunic covered a linen undershirt and could be unbuttoned at the wrists or collar for more room. One final piece of clothing made in the cottage was a sheepskin or woolen cloak that provided protection from wind and rain.

Clothes for women were made in the same manner, only styled differently. Over their linen undergown, or chemise, peasant women wore a warm woolen dress. Vests, which laced down the front, could also be worn over the dress to give it a more festive look.

House Cleaning

Medieval writers and artists convey a grim image of the interiors of cottages. Keeping them clean was a never-ending, laborious task. Interiors were dark because few cottages had windows, and those that did, did not have glass in them. The air hung heavy with the smoke from the hearth, where peat moss or wood was burned. One of the signs of affluence among villagers was the ability to afford dry wood that did not smoke as much as green wood, the only type of wood affordable to the very poor.

To keep the air moving, doors were often left open during the daytime. Although this helped clear the cottage air, it allowed children, chickens, and livestock to wander freely throughout. Floors were beaten earth covered with straw and were often mixed with animal dung. A few cottages of the wealthier families might have wood planking. One thirteenth-century writer, Hali Meidenhod, comments in his book *Lives of the Saints* that the village

Family Medicine

Most villagers had no concept of what caused disease, but most recognized the importance of a healthy diet. Lacking the ability to understand the causes of disease, such as germs and viruses, many debilitating diseases were viewed as God's way of punishing a person's sins.

Regardless of cause, caring for all illnesses fell to the woman of the family. If rest and warmth did not cure a suffering person, she turned to age-old customs involving locally gathered herbs. It was a common belief in medieval times that herbs steeped in wine alcohol would not only cure a variety of disease but also would aid digestive problems. Pure water for drinking was a luxury, so herbal infusions in wine became the norm. Common herbs used in wine infusions were angelica leaves, bergamot leaves, melissa herb, sage, mint, sweet woodruff leaves, and various flowers, including lavender and other fragrant plants.

If the family member failed to respond to herbal medicines, she turned to stronger natural remedies. The color of urine was known to reveal the basic functioning of the body, and medical manuscripts recommended different concoctions depending on the color, such as vinegar, sulfur, and various minerals. When such moderate remedies failed, women turned to more extreme ingredients, such as ground earthworms, gall from a castrated boar, sheep placentas, cow urine, and even animal excrement.

When all else failed, women might try bloodletting as a last resort. It was widely believed that bloodletting could restore a patient's health by balancing the fluids in his or her body. Bloodletting might be done by opening a vein in the patient's arm and removing a cup of blood or by applying locally found leeches, which would suck blood from the patient's arm.

During epidemics, when many in a village succumbed to diseases such as smallpox, the bubonic plague, or measles, nothing could be done but burn the bodies of the dead. Such widespread deaths triggered chilling rhymes, such as this one of unknown origin describing the red, circular skin rash of the bubonic plague, the posies that were funeral flowers, the ashes of cremation, and falling dead:

Ring around the rosie,
A pocketful of posie,
Ashes, Ashes,
All fall down.

wife who left the cottage for an hour or two was likely to encounter her home wrecked when she returned, finding "the cat at the bacon, and the dog at the hide [meat]. Her cake is burning on the stone [hearth] and the calf is licking up the milk. The pot is boiling over the fire."[25]

House cleaning was a matter of sweeping dirt, raking straw, and generally airing out the place. Brooms were made by wrapping two handfuls of straw or river reeds together at one end and attaching them to a stick. Water was so difficult to get and was so valuable for cleaning that none was wasted. Surfaces such as counters and tables were taken outside and cleaned with water left over from the weekly washing of clothes. Medieval wives preferred to clean house following the week's washing so the water could be used twice.

The picture painted by a thirteenth-century writer of the peasant housewife cleaning her cottage is indeed grim. One Sunday sermon, quoted by Frances and Joseph Gies in their book *Daily Life in Medieval Times,* comments on the work of wives: "She takes a broom and drives all the dirt of the house together; and, lest the dust rise . . . she casts it with great violence out the door. . . . On Saturday afternoon, she sweeps the house and casts all the dung and the filth behind the door in a heap."[26]

Milking Cows and Churning Butter

The responsibilities of village women sometimes extended beyond their children, family meals, and cottages. Poverty forced some women to work outside the home to generate additional income. Although many women worked as maids cleaning the homes of wealthier villagers, others earned money caring for milk cows. Milking the cows was one of the few farm jobs in the medieval village that was entirely within the purview of the women. These women were known as milkmaids. Not every village farmer kept cows because of the constant inconvenience of the milking, the need to find pasture for grazing, and the need for a place to milk them. Some milkmaids milked their cows inside the family cottage, but others milked them on the road just outside of the cottage.

Yet for those who did keep a cow or two, the family enjoyed the benefits. Fresh milk, cream, and butter were available to the family for meals or to trade for other family necessities. Butter was typically reserved for the wealthiest families in the village, and making it was a lengthy task.

The milkmaid first separated the heavy cream from the milk using butter strainers that were made of a material similar to gauze. The cream was then placed in a butter churn. The churn was a wooden cylinder that was two feet tall and tapered toward the top. The churn had a firm-fitting top with a small hole placed in the middle of it. Through the hole was placed a wooden churner that functioned as a plunger. The milkmaid rapidly forced the churner up and down until the cream gradually thickened into butter.

Life was tough, and milkmaids could cheat the public just as well as the miller or the baker, as this law indicates from the English village of Lynn:

> Milkwives are to sell good milk and cream that is sweet [i.e., not sour], in the form that it comes out of the cow— not combined or thickened with flour, nor diluted with water, to the deceit of the people, upon pain etc. And they are to sell good, sweet butter, freshly made.[27]

During the day, many milkmaids would join together at one cottage to churn their

A medieval drawing shows a milkmaid milking her cow. The cow also provided the medieval household with fresh cream, butter, and cheese.

butter. This provided the women an opportunity to sit together and talk while plunging the handles on their churners up and down as rapidly as possible. When children grew strong enough for this work, they too joined the churners' circle.

Children's Chores

In the peasant household, children provided valuable assistance to the family as early as five or six years of age. This assistance took the form of simple chores and did not take up a great deal of the child's time. As was the case with their fathers and mothers, the chores given to children reflected the general rule that males were responsible for outside agricultural work whereas females assumed responsibility for indoor domestic work.

Chores for boys between the ages of five and seven included fetching water; herding geese, sheep, or goats; gathering fruit, nuts, and firewood; walking and watering horses; and fishing. Chores for girls involved helping their mothers tend vegetable or herb gardens, make or mend clothes, churn butter, brew beer, and cook the meals. Older girls were often enlisted to care for, or at least watch over, their younger siblings.

A few families rented out their children to work in the homes of wealthier villagers. Boys might become valets, porters, or grooms for horses. Girls could be housemaids, nurses, or kitchen cleaners, called scullery maids. With a little training, young men and women might assist at skilled trades, including silk making, weaving, metalworking, brewing, or wine making. They might also acquire skills involved with milling, baking, and blacksmithing as well as helping in the fields.

The work done in the cottages was shared by all who did not work in the fields. Yet, at the end of the day, the entire family was able to come together for dinner, a few family activities, and finally a night's rest. These small cottages generated close family intimacy. Sharing two or three rooms at the most, family members knew each other's habits and business very well. For this reason, it was imperative that marriages function well and that the children he raised to assume their household responsibilities.

Marriage and the Family

Within the village community, the basic social and economic unit was the family. The family was nuclear, meaning it generally consisted of the two parents and their children. The size of the household tended to reflect the economic status of the household: The higher a family's income, the more children it was likely to have. Medieval historians share the opinion based on tax and court records that the number of people living under the typical cottage roof was rarely more than five or six.

However, the nuclear family sometimes expanded to take in extended family members. Size fluctuated as children died, aging grandparents moved in and stayed until they passed away, and cousins occasionally moved in as renters. Regardless of size or composition, all family members shared in all of the family's intimate details and participated in all ceremonies and rites of passage.

The most honored and celebrated of family traditions was marriage. More than simply an expression of love between a young man and woman, marriage represented the binding of two families, which everyone hoped would bring financial well-being to all involved. For this reason, marriages between adolescents in their late teens were not left to chance meetings.

Arranged Marriages

Most marriages during the Middle Ages were arranged by the family. This was true through-

out Europe, regardless of a person's wealth or social position, and tended to be truer among the upper class. The arranged marriage grew out of the need for families living in times of great economic uncertainty to conserve and consolidate wealth rather than to see it dissipate in a marriage to someone of a lower rank. This need motivated parents to seek spouses for their children with parents of a similar financial position and social status. Such arrangements did not mean that the two people who would marry did not know each other—they always did in a small village—it simply meant that they had little choice in the matter.

The negotiations between two families hoping to marry their children centered on the size of the dowry that the bride's family would present to the groom. The dowry was awarded to the groom as a marriage gift, but it functioned more subtly as an inducement to the groom's family to enter into the arrangement in the first place. Negotiations over the size and value of the dowry undermined some marriages and placed great strain on others. Yet dowries were the most important step in arranging the actual marriage.

The complexity of marriage negotiations was determined by the families' general wealth. A simple peasant dowry might be nonexistent in cases of severe poverty, but usually a prized ceramic mixing bowl or wooden chair was considered sufficient to satisfy the custom. The dowry for a villager who owned land and livestock required a more intricate dowry, which might include both land and livestock. Whatever the dowry might be, the final decision was not left to the two teenagers.

Marrying for love was usually out of the question, yet there is evidence that some arranged marriages were successful. Historians Joseph and Frances Gies point to the marriage of the fourteenth-century author Geoffrey de la Tour, who described his wife as "both fair and good, she was the bell and flower; and I delighted so much in her that I made for her love songs. But death, that on all makes war, took her from me. . . . But a true lover's heart never forgets the woman he has truly loved."[28]

Arranged marriages could also turn sour. Mismatches in age, interests, appearance, experiences, and other personal qualities sometimes undermined marriages. The motive of arranging a marriage for money or property did not always suit the bride and groom.

Like nearly all transactions of any sort in the medieval village, the lord of the manor charged a fee, called a *merchet,* for a marriage. The size of the *merchet* was generally determined by the size of the woman's dowry and whether she was marrying a man from another

This painting depicts a medieval peasant wedding ceremony. Most medieval marriages were arranged by the bride and groom's families.

In an agricultural setting, land was the major asset. But when a farmer died, his land could not be equally divided among his surviving sons. For this reason, all land was passed on to a single heir, always the firstborn son. This age-old tradition, extending back as far as the ancient Greeks, was called the right of primogenitor. The right of primogenitor intended to keep land in one single family. In cultures in which land was divided equally among all children or among all sons, the division of the land left each heir with so small a plot that it could not support one family.

The right of primogenitor had its drawbacks. Although this tradition kept landholdings in one piece, it also sometimes forced the firstborn son to postpone marriage until the family land passed into his hands on the death of his father or at the time of his father's retirement. This sometimes meant that the eldest son had few single women to pick from who were his

age. And sometimes the newlyweds might be too old to bear children.

Younger brothers were fortunate to be able to marry at a young age, but the right of primogenitor forced them to leave the farm to seek work elsewhere. Such a future created uncertainty depending upon the wealth of the family and its social position. A young man from a relatively wealthy village might receive a small amount of family money when he departed the village during his late teens; this sum would help support him until he could find work. Available jobs included working as a professional soldier, as a clergy member, or possibly purchasing a small piece of land or a business. The secondborn son of a poor family did not fare as well. His options were limited to working as a day laborer, perhaps working for his older bother but never owning his own farm, or, worst of all, sliding into the class of vagabonds and criminals that wandered from village to village begging and stealing to stay alive.

village, which would increase the cost. Whatever the cost, haggling played a part in it, as one father was told by a steward of a lord: "Make the best bargain you can."[29] Once the financial and legal negotiations had been completed, the bride and groom were notified of their marriage, a date was set, and the families and friends gathered for the ceremony.

The Wedding Ceremony

Determining what constituted a marriage during most of the Middle Ages was a tricky proposition. The only rule for a marriage was a very general consent on the part of the bride and the groom that they both wanted to get

married, followed by the consummation of the marriage. The consent could be made at one of the couple's home, at the village church, or outdoors somewhere in the village—little more was required. Even the church required nothing more than a marriage being public and the groom receiving a dowry—it did not even require the wedding ceremony be held in a church or that a priest preside over it.

Local custom, not law, made the local village church the favorite place for weddings in France and England; however, taverns and woodlands were more popular in Germany. Either a priest or a family friend conducted the very simple ceremony. During the late Middle Ages, when the wedding ceremony had become standardized, village weddings followed a ritual that only varied slightly from country to country.

When all guests had arrived, the master of ceremony asked whether the bride and groom were of proper kinship, meaning they were not related or at least they were not too closely related. In small villages, avoiding marrying one's cousin, for example, was at times difficult. Next, the dowry was announced, and the bridegroom gave the bride a small bag of coins to disperse to the poor, who always gathered at weddings in anticipation of this handout. A simple ring was then produced by the bridegroom, which he placed on the fourth finger of her left hand as tradition dictated. According to a fourteenth-century priest, the fourth finger was chosen because, "as doctors say, there is a vein coming from the heart of a woman to the fourth finger, and therefore the ring is put on the same finger, so that she should keep unity and love with him, and he with her."[30]

Vows were then spoken, and the party set off to a home or a local tavern for a feast that included "bride ale"—a specially brewed ale served at weddings—and a variety of food specially prepared for the party. In most villages, tradition required the married couple to invite the servants of the manor to the wedding feast.

A marriage ceremony in a German village had a slightly different twist. Following the wedding vows, the groom stepped on the foot of his new bride, as is recorded in this thirteenth-century description of the marriage between a man named Lämmerslint and his bride, Gotelind:

> They gave away thus Gotelind
> To be the wife of Lämmerslint,
> And thus they gave young Lämmerslint
> To be the man of Gotelind.
> And now they sang, the questions put,
> And Lämmerslint trod her on the foot.[31]

The custom mentioned in the last line, which refers to the groom stepping on the bride's foot, is the subject of considerable debate among historians. Most historians believe that it symbolizes an old custom associated with the seizure of property. Others, however, do not believe that to be the case.

Childbirth

For most of the medieval villagers, the prime purpose of marriage was not so much to create a love relationship for the rest of their lives as it was to produce children. So important was childbirth for all social classes that a failure to produce children within one or two years following a marriage was of great concern not only to the newlyweds but to the entire village as well. This concern was reflected by references to childless women as needing to be "cured" by someone other than the husband. One German village, which recorded many of its customs at the church, endorsed the custom of finding another man to impregnate the wife:

> Send your wife to the next annual fair in the vicinity, and see that she is cleanly dressed and has adorned herself. She should also be given a purse with plenty of money so that she could treat herself to something; and if she returned home without being cured it was only for the devil to help her.[32]

The birth of a child was greeted with great joy in the medieval village. Childbirth took place at home, without men, and with considerable fear for the lives of the mother and child. Thousands of coroner reports that have survived reveal high mortality rates for birthing mothers and their babies because of

A midwife hands a newborn child to an attendant in this fourteenth-century painting. Only women were present for the birth of a child in most medieval households.

the many complications, such as excessive bleeding, for which there were no medical remedies. In one German village the infant mortality was nearly 13 percent. For this reason, baptism of newborns near death was often done on the spot rather than waiting until the mother and child had stabilized.

Fear of an unbaptized child dying and its soul going to hell was very real during the Middle Ages. Midwives, the local women who assisted in the delivery, often kept a bowl of water handy to use to baptize the baby. If the midwife encountered complications during the delivery, suggesting the baby was dying, she summoned the priest. However, she might perform the baptism herself if the baby was near death. Accounts exist of midwives baptizing a baby the moment its head

emerged and, in even more extreme conditions, when the mother had already died, actually cutting open the mother to baptize the baby before it too died.

When a delivery was successful, the newborn was washed, swaddled, and presented to the awaiting family members. After a day or two at most, the baby was taken to the church for a formal baptism and a name was chosen. Only a handful of first names for boys and girls was used, and typically the name chosen was that of the parent or grandparent.

Childhood

All babies were nursed by their mothers, even though some mothers had to return to their work on the farms or in the village shops. During the day, if both parents were away, the baby was typically cared for by a grandparent, a young babysitter, or possibly an older sibling. Coroner reports indicate that the mortality rate during the first year of life was very low in comparison to birth.

Young children spent most of their time imitating their parents. From a young age children were expected to learn the tasks that enabled them to help their parents. Girls typically played in or around the house, helping to stir the soup kettle, adding small sticks of wood to the fire, drawing water from the village well, mending a tear in a shirt, or collect-

ing vegetables. Young boys got up at dawn with their fathers and followed them out to the fields to learn how to hitch the oxen to the plow, take a sack of wheat to the mill for grinding, or string a bow and notch an arrow. Play involved simple objects such as building a castle with sticks and rocks, taking an old piece of bread to a stream and sailing it as if it were a boat, or wielding a small tree branch as a sword.

The transition from childhood to adolescence brought a lot of change for both boys and girls. Unlike the fun they may have enjoyed when they were younger and trailing along with their parents, adolescents were assigned chores that they were expected to

In this medieval painting a child gathers wood shavings from the floor in his parents' carpentry shop.

learn and to execute in a responsible manner. As was the case during their earlier years, the chores for the girls involved tasks around the house while the boys went to the fields. Completing their chores lasted until about fifteen or sixteen, when both boys and girls were expected to transition into the adult life of full-time work and greater responsibility.

The sole exception to this routine occurred in the poorest of families, where adolescents were sent to the homes of wealthier families to begin their lives as servants. They usually worked as field hands or in the house. Although their wages were low, the family for whom they worked fed and housed them and sent their wages back home to their parents.

Whatever the nature of childhood might have been, it was short. For the babies who survived birth, adolescence, and moved into adulthood during their late teens, they had reached half of their life expectancy, which averaged just forty-five years.

Old Age and Death

As villagers grew older, diseases and work-related accidents took their toll, especially for those involved all of their lives in hard, physical work. At any moment a horse might trample and crush a plowman's knee, harvesters working in close quarters and swinging sharp sickles sometimes suffered debilitating accidental stabbings, and all men took their chances from time to time fighting in the armies of their lords.

The Village Priest

The priest, sometimes called a parson, was appointed to the village church by the lord. Even though he was a member of the clergy, he had a similar relationship to the lord as did other villagers. The primary responsibility of the priest was to minister to the spiritual needs of the villagers during major ceremonies, such as baptisms, marriages, and last rites. The priest also delivered the Sunday sermon and was active in organizing church functions that played a major role in the social lives of village families.

There was one circumstance, however, where the priest could exercise considerable power and authority over a villager's life. Open violation of basic rules of religious conduct on the part of a parishioner could compel the priest to recommend to his superiors the excommunication of a parishioner. Excommunication was a final punishment that banished the offending parishioner from the church. Such a judg-

ment was so severe in small villages that the punishment carried over to secular life and effectively banished the person from all village activities as well.

Except for his religious obligations, the priest's life was similar to the other officials appointed by the lord. The priest was obligated to pay rent to the lord and to be available for private services in the manor house. In order to pay his rent and meet other personal obligations, the priest in turn levied demands on the villagers, just as the lord did. The village priest at Ramsey, England, for example, is recorded to have occasionally requested his parishioners to provide him with bread, beef, flour, ale, lard, beans, butter, bacon, honey, lamb, chickens, eggs, and cheese. In addition to these goods, he also required cash from the offering plate to purchase horses, clothes, wall hangings, candlesticks, and dinner plates.

A twelfth-century painting shows villagers burying plague victims. Disease was a common cause of death in the middle ages.

When older workers were no longer capable of plowing fields and cutting hay, they turned to the younger generation for assistance until their deaths. In many cases, parents would give their children their land in exchange for their support. This exchange was arranged in the form of a signed legal document or, in some cases, simply in the form of verbal promises. In either case, the agreement typically stipulated that the children would maintain their parents in a separate dwelling or perhaps a separate room in their home without charging any fee. One such agreement specified, "A room at the end of the house that has food, fuel, and clothing and also a place by the fire."[33]

If an elderly couple had no children, a pension could be arranged with a young local villager. Such pensions were especially common in regions that had experienced epidemics or wars that killed thousands of people. Written contracts stipulated an exchange of land and home to a young villager for annual contributions of money, clothing, and food to the elderly until they died. In 1332 one such pension specified what an elderly man should receive each year: "One new garment with a hood, worth 3 shillings 4 pence, two pairs of linen sheets, three pairs of new shoes, one pair of new socks, and victuals in food and drink as decently as is proper."[34]

The daily activities for the elderly typically depended on whether they lived with their children and whether they had grandchildren. For those who were grandparents, much of their day was spent looking after the grandchildren and taking them to the central village square, where they spent part of the day with other grandparents babysitting their grandchildren. Sunday became an important day for the elderly as well. In the morning they attended church services, and in the afternoon they attended a local festival, where they could play games such as tenpin, a simple game similar to bowling; checkers; and chess; or they could watch one of the many

Marriage and the Family **63**

sporting events that took place in local fields or on the water.

When death was imminent, the village priest was summoned to administer last rites. If the person was so ill and weak that he or she could not speak or respond, last rites were automatically administered. If, on the other hand, the person was coherent, he or she was asked whether the priest should proceed. Many did not want last rites if they thought that they had a chance to recover; it was believed that surviving after receiving last rites was bad luck. If death did occur, however, the body was immediately taken either to the person's home or to the church.

Medieval tradition required a wake to commemorate each death. Wakes were typically held at the house of the deceased in the presence of the decedent's body. Friends and family gathered, talked directly to the decedent, shared jokes with him or her as if still alive, and consumed food and ale. These wakes became so notorious for degrading into drunken fests that one fourteenth-century preacher complained that those attending wakes behave "like madmen who make merry at our death, and attend our burying for an ale."[35]

Following the wake, the body was carried to the church, where it was sewn into a grain sack and was draped with a black shroud. After a funeral mass was said, the body was placed in a simple wooden casket—or none at all in the case of the poor—and placed in the earth.

Old age for those who were both childless and poor was a double misfortune. Without work, land, children, or money, little assistance was given and certainly no pensions were granted. The elderly who found themselves in this unfortunate circumstance were at the mercy of everyone. Some were fortunate to get an occasional meal from the local church, but not much else. Many were forced in their pathetic straits to wander from village to village as beggars until they finally died, perhaps one night when the first frost arrived in autumn or when they simply threw themselves from a bridge.

Inheritance

Upon a person's death, medieval customs as well as inheritance laws specified the disposition of the decedent's money, personal possessions, and property. Inheritance could be a complicated matter depending upon who died and who laid claims to inheritance. Whatever a person's wealth or status, inheritance was a matter of interest to family members as well as to the village lord.

Inheritance laws varied widely throughout Europe yet generally followed established customs. When a young married man with children died, most of his holdings went to his widow, which would then become her dowry when she remarried. If, however, he was old and his children were grown, most of his property would transfer directly to the children, who would then be required to look after their mother.

Medieval custom established that, upon the death of a man, the lord of a manor had a right to a heriot, a death tax that was paid in some commodity. It was not unusual following a funeral to see the lord arrive at the house of the deceased. There, in front of family mourners, he entered the cottage and selected one valuable item, such as a table or a bed, and would carry it away. The heriot was determined by the amount of land owned by the deceased. One French court ruled that the widow of a deceased farmer who owned no ox, sheep, horse, or any other major asset, had to hand over "the best cloth or grain which ever will please him [the lord] the more."[36] In 1348 the village of Langley, England, recorded a total of eighty-six heriots: twenty-two horses, seventeen cows, eight bulls, five sheep, thirty-two insignificant items such as a hoe or a milk pitcher, and two heriot entries that simply read, "nothing because they were poor."[37]

Widows

Life for a widow was particularly difficult. Widows had rights in the medieval village, but they were not equal to those of a widower. Inheritance laws typically allowed a widow to inherit only between one-half and one-third of her husband's personal assets, such as money and household items, but all of his land. Fearing that a widow would be incapable of producing a good crop, the lord of the manor often pressured her to remarry as quickly as possible. The lord's concern was not so much for the welfare of the widow as it was for his share of the crop or the taxes he collected on it. Historians Frances and Joseph Gies, in their book *Daily Life in Medieval Times*, point out that "widows' rights, and inheritance customs in general, were influenced by the long term fluctuations in availability of land. The scarcer land became, the more attractive a widow became."[38]

In spite of difficulties for most widows, historians also point out that some widows often had more control over their lands and homes after their husbands' deaths than before. In the Middle Ages, when land meant wealth, widowed women could use the wealth land gave them in much the same manner as the men did. A widow could use the income from her holdings to purchase goods, or she could sell the land for a single lump sum of money.

This medieval widow may have enjoyed more control over her land and home after her husband's death.

For those widows who did not remarry, the church offered some degree of assistance. During the Middle Ages religious institutions became open to women who were willing to work for the church either by providing maintenance or by charity work within the village. The church offered women the same support as it did for men in terms of some small amount of prestige. Such support, especially for the poor, included occasional meals, perhaps a place to sleep, and a chance at performing a useful civic function.

Just as hard work and early death were accepted and understood as part of medieval life, so too was the need to find occasional relaxation and enjoyment. Much like all other aspects of village life, leisure moments were simple, of short duration, and of little cost.

Time off from the family chores and tedium of the workplace left precious little time for relaxation. Saturday night and part of Sunday presented most villagers with one day, at most, to take their minds off their daily struggles. The need for diversion was so great that Sunday presented everyone with a variety of simple yet entertaining distractions. For those devoutly committed to the church, Sunday morning was dedicated to attending matins, or morning services.

Sunday Church Services

For those choosing to attend church—perhaps half of the population of a village—it was expected that they would bathe and dress in clean clothes long before the church bells rang. Sunday did not excuse anyone from the chores of milking cows, feeding chickens, and cleaning manure from the barn, but no one attended services smelling like the barn. Those attending arrived in time to enter and find their seats; like any other social gathering in the village, those occupying the best seats—the ones up front—were the families owning the most land and livestock.

The authority and influence of the village church fluctuated over time. "One of the primary points to remember about the church in the Middle Ages," says historian Sherrilyn Kenyon in *The Writer's Guide to Everyday Life in the Middle Ages,* "is that its policy and

A medieval painting shows villagers taking part in a baptism as a part of Sunday church services.

power changed drastically and rapidly. There were times when the church's power was weak and other times when it was strong."[39] Whether strong or weak, many villagers attended and respectfully listened to the sermon, took communion, and taught their children church rituals and ceremony.

The sermon was the priest's opportunity to address his congregation on issues of concern to him. In this regard, his lessons reminded illiterate parishioners of the teachings of Christ, of their spiritual obligations to avoid going to hell, and of their financial obligations to the church and the village lord. The priest's sermons often reflected the influence of the lord in the reminders that told even the poorest not to neglect their debt, regardless of how significant it might be.

Following the service, many families spent the rest of the day at the church taking part in family activities such as games for children and potluck lunches. It also allowed adults the opportunity to discuss the progress of their crops and animals and personal matters such as family health, weddings, and deaths.

For some villagers, attending church was a tough decision because, with just one day away from the farm, other village activities could not be enjoyed. One of the favorites that competed with the church was the marketplace that often operated Sunday morning.

The Marketplace

Some people were fortunate to live in a village that allowed a marketplace. This was the principal site for buying and selling vegetables, meats, and other daily necessities as well as silly trinkets. Goods were sold only in

The Village Charter

All villages offered a variety of diversions, but not all offered the same ones. The way of life in every European village, whether in England, Spain, Sweden, France, or Germany, was largely defined by its royal charter issued by the king. Charters defined such things as the lands included within the village boundaries, customs that could be practiced, legal jurisdictions, and obligations to which the townsfolk were subject or from which they were exempted.

Charters also specified local rules for each village. For example, a charter might grant permission to hold one major fair each year, to set up a central marketplace one day a week, brew ale, catch and keep all big fish, hunt small animals, and sell wines.

Villagers' financial fortunes were also affected by charters. If the king was well disposed toward the village at the time he issued the charter, he might exempt the villagers from tolls on merchandise, taxes owed to him, inheritance laws specifying money paid to the lord of the manor, and on the toll to cross local bridges. In 1403, for example, according to the website Medieval English Towns, the king of England modified the village charter of Maldon by granting the villagers the following prosperities and exempting several tolls, taxes, and rents:

The Moothall [town hall]; All vacant plots of land in the town; Rents from market stalls; Portman Marsh and the fees for pasturage there; Hawgable [labor services] rents; Toltray [a toll on ships carrying cargoes of salt]; Landchepe [a tax on the sale of any property within the village].

the morning until about one o'clock, when the ringing of the town bell signaled the market's close. Choosing Sunday morning to open the marketplace often angered the local priest because the market was often more popular than Sunday's sermon.

Vendors arrived early and set up temporary wooden stalls to display their goods, and they used colorful pennants to attract shoppers' attention. The site took on the look of a colorful social event as townspeople perused the goods while children and dogs ran throughout the market enjoying their temporary freedom. The local poor offered to cut the hair of an entire family for a penny or to sell extra pails of milk. Horses too old to plow were auctioned off to the butchers, and colorful beads, threads, and fabrics were sold.

Buyers made offers on goods, and their haggling over prices could be heard throughout the marketplace. Some came just for the fun of seeing the crowds, others to try their luck at illegal gambling. Some vendors offered games of cards and dice set up on card tables that could be disassembled hastily. Others came hoping to find some simple items such as pepper, honey, and good-quality leather for belts and shoes.

Each village had its own rules governing the marketplace. Rules stipulated who could trade and sell goods, where traders and sellers could set up their stalls, the hours of the marketplace, and what goods could be sold and traded. One German village with a history of violence created the following rule in an attempt to avoid further violence: "Let them not bring arms or breastplates to sell. And if they be found carrying them, let all their goods be taken from them, one half to the share of the palace, but the other half shall be divided between the finders."[40]

Sometimes marketplace rules had international repercussions. In 1242, for example, friction between the French and English prompted the French king to ban Englishmen from trading their goods at French village marketplaces. According to an English document, "This dishonorable and cruel proceeding soon reached the ears as well as the feelings of the king of England, on which he also gave orders that the French traders found in any part of England should undergo a just retaliation."[41]

Regardless of the rules, some village folks were generally too poor to do much more than enjoy the sights, sounds, and smells of the marketplace. Their poverty, coupled with their low social status, also excluded them from many forms of sports and entertainment enjoyed by the nobility, such as hunting, jousting, and polo, all of which required a horse. Despite these few restrictions, there were still plenty of other activities available to everyone.

Many of the favorites were the simplest and the cheapest. Some activities, such as foot races, wrestling, swimming, and boxing, were popular and cost nothing. The most popular sport, however, because it involved many people both as participants and as spectators, was soccer.

Soccer

Soccer was a widely played game in medieval Europe. Few written descriptions of soccer can be found, yet a number of drawings and paintings depict the sport. These drawings show soccer to have been a game played with a leather ball stuffed with straw, rags, or some other type of wadded-up material. The game was popular in the villages because the only cost was the ball, and according to some early accounts, even that cost was sometimes sidestepped by using round baskets stuffed with wet straw.

Spectators and players alike enjoy a soccer game played in a large market square in this medieval painting.

Games were played either in a large market square or in an open field. The market square was a favorite venue because it was usually flat, with well-packed dirt, and large crowds naturally gravitated to the open area. The drawback, however, was the inevitable result that the mayhem of the game spilled out onto the city streets. When carts of food and merchants' tents were occasionally knocked over, protests might force the village lord or bailiff to ban the game.

Local teams often took to the fields to play each other as well as teams from neighboring villages. The enthusiasm for the game was so intense that everyone wishing to play was allowed on the field. Rather than a well-organized and well-coordinated game, men and women numbering in the hundreds took to the field to take part in a chaotic game that

sent many from the field with bloody noses and split lips. Some of these contests knew no bounds; when the number of participants numbered over one hundred, some soccer fields extended far across the landscape.

On occasion, fields of wheat or vegetable patches were ripped apart by trampling soccer hordes. The situation became so bad that in 1314 the following ban was issued by one village:

And whereas there is a great uproar in the village through certain tumults arising from the striking of great footballs in the field of the public—from which many evils perchance may arise—which may God forbid—we do command and do forbid, on the King's behalf, upon pain of imprisonment, that such games shall not be practiced henceforth within this village.[42]

For those who enjoyed sporting events but found soccer to be too violent, other forms of less violent sports were available. The proximity of villages to rivers encouraged many forms of water sports, the most popular being water jousting.

Water Jousting

Poverty prevented most villagers from taking part in the popular aristocratic sport of horse jousting. The cost of outfitting a horse and purchasing a full suit of armor for the rider was beyond the means of most villagers. To make up for their inability to participate in the sport yet indulge their love of it, villagers took to boats in their local rivers to enjoy a very similar sport: water jousting.

The sport of water jousting appears to have enjoyed wide popularity during the Middle Ages. Its earliest accounts appear in twelfth-century French manuscripts, and references to the sport continue all the way through the fifteenth century. Water jousts were generally held as part of various civic festivals during the summer months, with local teams competing against each other or against the boat of a neighboring village.

Water jousting resembled the jousting of two knights on horseback charging at each other. Instead of knights mounted on charg-

Two knights charge at each other in a jousting tournamnet. Jousting was the sport of wealthy aristocrats and village peasants were forced to find alternative activities.

A Moral Objection to the Village Marketplace

In 1250 Humbert de Romans, a writer for the church, wrote a treatise on the marketplace that was widely enjoyed on Sunday throughout thousands of European villages. Quoted in Roy C. Cave and Herbert H. Coulson's book *A Source Book for Medieval Economic History*, de Romans presents his views on why he believes the marketplace was a place of immoral activity:

Though markets and fairs are terms often used indiscriminately, there is a difference between them, for fairs deal with larger things and only once in the year, or at least rarely in the same place, and to them come men from afar. But markets are for lesser things, the daily necessaries of life; they are held weekly and only people from near at hand come. Hence markets are usually morally worse than fairs. They are held on feast days, and men miss thereby the divine office and the sermon and even disobey the precept of hearing Mass, and attend these

meetings against the Church's commands. Sometimes, too, they are held in graveyards and other holy places. Frequently you will hear men swearing there: "By God I will not give you so much for it," or "By God I will not take a smaller price," or "By God it is not worth so much as that." Sometimes again the lord is defrauded of market dues, which is perfidy and disloyalty. . . . Sometimes, too, quarrels happen and violent disputes. . . . Drinking is occasioned. . . . Christ, you may note, was found in the market-place, for Christ is justice and justice should be there. . . . Thus the legend runs of a man who, entering an abbey, found many devils in the cloister but in the market-place found but one, alone on a high pillar. This filled him with wonder. But it was told him that in the cloister all is arranged to help souls to God, so many devils are required there to induce monks to be led astray, but in the market, place, since each man is a devil to himself, only one other demon suffices.

ers, water jousters set out on local rivers in long, thin rowboats with a team of eight to twelve oarsmen. A jouster stood on a small wooden platform on the boat's stern wielding a long pole with a blunted end. The objective of the tournament was for the jouster to knock his opponent, who was similarly armed, into the water.

With the banks of the river lined with spectators wagering on their favorite boat, the two boats rowed to opposite positions on the river. When separated by a hundred yards or so, the sound of the starter's horn set the two boats in motion toward each other. The rowers tried to maneuver to give their jouster the best possible position as the two boats approached each other amid the shouts and

cheering of the spectators. If both jousters missed on the first pass, the boats turned around for another attempt. Eventually, one of the jousters ended up in the river, thoroughly soaked but rarely injured. Tournaments might last a matter of minutes or, if the jousters were unsuccessful, for as long as half an hour when many passes were needed.

Archery

Water jousting was a recreational sport that had little value beyond the enjoyment of the contestants and the spectators. The same could not be said, however, for the sport of archery. The ability to hit the bull's-eye of a target in competition might be translated into a critical test of survival on the battlefield.

Archery was one of the favorite medieval sports associated with warfare. Village peasants could not afford the horse and armor needed to fight as knights, but they were required to report for battle as archers anytime the lord of the village summoned them. Consequently, it behooved the lord in each village to support archery competitions because they not only provided entertainment for the local folk, but they also honed the skills of his foot soldiers.

The use of the bow and arrow for warfare predated medieval Europe by several thousand years. One of the most famous artistic historical documents, the Bayeux Tapestry, depicts archers and other warriors fighting during the Norman Invasion of England in 1066. In battle, the archers typically took up positions behind the knights and shot their arrows hundreds of yards into the phalanx, or formation, of the onrushing soldiers to disrupt and break up their orderly advance.

Archery contests honed the accuracy of the village men obligated for defense of the village. During some periods, most able-bodied men were required to practice at least once a week on Sunday after church. All villages kept straw-filled targets that were set up against the stairs or walls of the church. As might be expected, archers took pride in their accuracy, and contests were inevitable. To further encourage practice, targets on wheels were rolled down lawns, and the lord regularly offered small monetary rewards for the best shooting.

Of equal importance to accuracy was distance. Village archers also practiced shooting at a forty-five degree angle as far as possible and as rapidly as possible. Good archers were capable of distances up to three hundred yards, and, more important, they were able to shoot ten arrows a minute. Although an army of one hundred archers might exhaust its supply of arrows in four minutes, it would be capable of showering four thousand arrows in a concentrated area.

Animal Baiting

Archery and other sports that simulated military tactics were too passive for some villagers. For them, one of the more gruesome forms of entertainment was bearbaiting. This form of amusement typically involved a man who traveled from village to village with a bear and a pack of three or four dogs. The man then performed one or two types of bearbaiting: either wrestling the bear or chaining the bear to a post and then setting a pack of crazed hounds loose on the animal.

Bear wrestling was a relatively harmless act between the bear owner and his animal. Typically a muzzle was placed over the bear's mouth while the man and the animal wrestled on a dirt ring to the screams and cheers of the crowd. The owner put on an act of struggling for his life with the bear until he was finally able to escape, often dramatizing his fear of the animal by running into the crowd and asking for help. Although everyone understood this was an act and was simply for fun, some of these traveling bear wrestlers were missing a hand or an arm. One English newspaper carried the following story explaining missing limbs:

> As a lame man was lately shewing tricks with a bear, over against Suffolk-street, the creature being hungry, or ill-humour'd, shew'd his master such a trick as was like to have cost him his life, for his muzzle being somewhat loose, he bit him grievously by his stump-hand, and with

his paws tore his arm and face in a sad manner.[43]

Following ten or fifteen minutes of bear wrestling, the bear was then chained to a heavy post set in the ground, and his muzzle was removed. This was the start of the gruesome part of entertainment that packed the temporary benches that were set up in a ring around the bear. Next the owner of the bear released the three or four hounds that were trained to attack the bear with the ferocity of trying to kill it.

The bloody spectacle began with the snarling dogs throwing themselves at the bear, biting and ripping at the chained animal. The dogs never killed the bear; that would have put the owner out of business, but they often bit it ferociously on the nose and neck, causing it to bleed profusely. As for the dogs, the loss of a leg usually killed most of them, although on occasion a swipe by the bear's claw ripped the poor animal open, sending it flying into the crowd to the delight of everyone.

Dancing

Men enjoyed more than war activities, physical sports, and gruesome fights between dogs and bears. They also enjoyed joining with their

A medieval artist portrays a lively scene of medieval villagers drinking and dancing. Dancing was one of the most common forms of medieval village entertainment.

wives and girlfriends in social activities. Dancing was one of the most popular forms of entertainment because it was enjoyed by all village groups—young and old, men and women, and rich and poor. Dancing took place among small numbers of persons celebrating birthdays and weddings in private homes, on many of the religious holidays at the local parish church, at annual functions held at the manor house for those invited by the lord, and at open-air dances at the village square. The most favored by the townsfolk were those held at the square. Open to any one, dancers turned out in large numbers because, unlike the other smaller dances, this one would have music by traveling bands of troubadours.

The dances most commonly described during the early Middle Ages were those involving large groups rather than a couple. Favorite types of dances were ring dances, so named because dancers held hands, formed a ring, and danced in a circle. Dancers also enjoyed chain dances. These were similar to the ring dances in that everyone held hands, but they were more free-form, allowing the chain leader to weave around the floor followed by the rest of the dancers.

Later during the Middle Ages a new trend in dancing began in northern Italy. This new form began as a traditional group dance but then changed when couples paired off to dance with each other. This new form of dancing was at first considered risqué and immoral by many parents, but it became popular and quickly spread to France and Germany. In time, this form of dance added both a fast tempo, called a *bassadanza*, and a slow one, called a *ballo*.

Slow dancing eventually became the favorite for young people who were dating. They liked the idea of showing off and the intimacy of dancing with just one partner. Unfortunately for them, many parish churches objected to the dancing because they considered it devil worship and put a stop to it.

The Village Tavern

The village tavern was another place where both men and women could enjoy each other's company. The tavern might be a genuine place for drinking ale and enjoying a small meal, or it might simply be the house of anyone who had recently brewed a batch of ale. Whichever the case might have been, villagers met to socialize, play games, and generally forget life's difficulties.

Laws governing the sale of ale were few because ale was so widely consumed not by only men and women but by young adults as well. The reason for such widespread consumption was more a matter of health than inebriation. Ale was one of the few drinks that required boiling in the distillation process, which made it safer to drink than local water since that often carried various microscopic organisms such as amoebas that caused severe cases of dysentery. Nonetheless, most villages and towns passed some laws regulating the consumption of ale on Sundays, such as this one from the village of Maldon, England, warning, "Any brewer who sends ale from his house to gannokers [ale houses] on Sundays at the time of matins [morning services], mass or other divine service, shall be fined 12d."[44]

Excessive drinking was an acknowledged and widespread problem. In 1276 a coroner in the village of Estow, England, reported in his records that "Osbert le Wuayl, son of William Christmasse, coming home at midnight drunk and disgustingly over-fed after an evening in Bedford, fell and struck his head on a stone breaking the whole of his head."[45] Besides the unfortunate end to this fellow, the same coroner reported other

This sixteenth-century painting shows villagers enjoying a jug of ale and a meal at the local tavern.

deaths as a result of too much drink. Some of these reports included a man who fell off his horse riding home from a tavern; one who, in a drunken state, fell into a well and drowned; and a third who, while relieving himself in a pond, fell in and drowned. Yet the strangest report of a death as a result of drunkenness was a man who was carrying a pot of ale down the village street when a dog bit him. While trying not to spill his ale as he picked up a stone to hurl at the dog, the man tripped and struck his head on a stone wall, killing him.

Despite the various laws, accidents and violence resulting from too much ale were common occurrences along with other, more deliberate forms of criminal activity. With only a bailiff to enforce laws and protect the citizenry, every member of the village was called on from time to time to participate actively in village justice.

Although crimes of various sorts were common occurrences, prisons did not exist in the medieval village. Lacking the ability to lock up violators of local law and custom, the medieval village dealt with offenders in a variety of other ways, some of which involved the courts but many that did not. A manorial court under the jurisdiction of the lord oversaw all legal matters concerning the village, with the exception of major crimes such as murder. The lord of the manor or a jury of twelve landholders held ultimate resolution of all court cases.

Manorial courts were fairly informal, meeting at the manor house, outdoors under a large tree, or in some public place. Typical disputes involved trespassing on a man's land, questions about boundary lines, maintenance

A lord of a manor acts as judge in a scene from a medieval book on crime and law.

of fences, debts, and violations of contracts. The process was intentionally kept so simple that if the accused could find several men who would attest to his innocence, he was released.

Crime committed by village locals usually amounted to relatively innocuous offenses, such as poaching game in the lord's forest, petty theft, local businessmen cheating customers, and occasional violence usually linked to drunkenness. Crimes committed by outsiders, however, could sometimes become more severe.

Poaching

Poaching large game and valuable trees was illegal yet widespread. Laws restricted the illegal hunting of major forest animals such as deer and boars as well as the taking of certain large trees. Such laws favored the nobility, who recognized that the forest was the place where their game animals—a source of sport rather than food—resided and foraged. These laws, however, did not deter villagers from occasionally dressing in brown and green clothing to match the brush and wandering into the lord's forests in search of game or trees. The only motive for poaching among local villagers was basic subsistence: Poaching supported their daily needs for food and fuel for fires.

Local villagers had some rights when it came to the forest, such as gathering dead twigs and fallen branches, hunting small mammals such as rabbits and squirrels, and collecting birds' eggs to feed their families. But these rights were felt by the poor to be too limited, and a great temptation existed to make use of the forest's larger four-legged animals and trees to supplement their families' need for food and wood.

Poachers sometimes risked capture by entering the forest at sunrise or sunset to trap and kill a deer. This sort of activity was so common that local lords paid sheriffs to act as game wardens. Capture brought a severe penalty. The most famous poacher in English history, whether real or a folk hero, was Robin Hood, who allegedly began his life of crime during the thirteenth century when the sheriff of Nottingham saw him kill one of the king's royal deer in Sherwood Forest.

Yet according to local court records, poachers always had the sympathies of the other villagers and were rarely caught. When they were, however, some were clamped in the stocks, and others were fined. Court records from Wrenthrop, England, for May 1277 report that "Robert the Mower was seized and imprisoned three months for a deer, which his dogs . . . choked in the fields of Wyruthorpe." Twenty years later the same court records report that "William de Lewynthorpe and others fined 8s. 4d. killed a doe in Wyruthorpe field."[46]

Poaching large hardwood trees also brought heavy fines. In 1332 the court rolls show that

John son of Amabilla on 1 October 1331, cut down and took an ash tree worth 10s. [10 pennies] in Wyruthorpe in a place called Arkelyerd to his damage. . . . And John therefore he is to pay principal and damages, and be amerced [compensated] 3d. [3 shillings = 36 pennies].[47]

Thieving

Poaching was waved off as being inconsequential by most peasant villagers because only the village lord and his noble friends were harmed. Stealing from other villagers, however, was not casually dismissed. Thieving often occurred when unemployed vagabonds wandered aimlessly from town to town robbing homes and merchants or when pick-pockets working in pairs mingled at fairs and stole coin purses from villagers. Such forms of thieving were casually tolerated, but the form of thievery that was not acceptable was when one villager stole from another.

Thieving between neighbors was a social ill that permeated the lives of all villagers. It was particularly heinous because the victim and perpetrator usually knew each other; when a thief was revealed to the village, it tainted the personal relationships of all because of the suspicions it cast on everyone. Losses could be devastating because most villagers had so little to lose. Although the lord was charged with the enforcement of laws,

A peasant protects his home from a band of thieves. Formal law enforcement was virtually nonexistent in the medieval village.

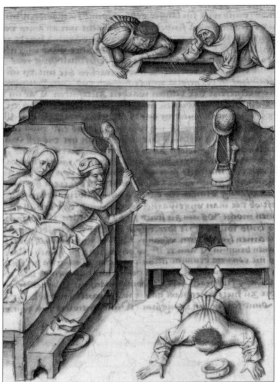

common villagers and farmers had to look out for their own interests by keeping an eye on their neighbors and friends.

Farmers were constantly on the lookout for other farmers who might steal one of their furrows, a pig, sheep, chicken, or even manure from the manure pile that was typically found next to each farmer's cottage or barn. The small size of the sheaves of wheat made them a tempting object for theft. Historians Frances and Joseph Gies, in their book *Daily Life in Medieval Times,* point out that favorite places to hide stolen sheaves were "bosoms, tunics, boots, or pockets or sacks hidden near the grange [field]."[48] Theft became such a problem during the harvest season that it finally forced many villages to outlaw any farming activities at night to discourage such illicit activities.

Nonagricultural villagers also suffered losses. Food was commonly stolen from shop owners such as bakers. Thieves also stole from homes because the windows of cottages did not have glass and they were easily entered. Leaving foods suspended outside during the winter, a common way of preserving perishables, also had its risks. The Gieses relate the story of a thief who robbed a village house and then self-inflicted his own punishment: "One thief became a victim of his own crime when he climbed a ladder to purloin a ham hanging from a roof beam. When the householder, Matilda Bolle, saw him leaving and gave the alarm, he panicked and tumbled from the ladder, and died of a broken neck."[49]

Raising the Hue and Cry

The reporting of a crime and pursuit of a criminal began with the calling out of the hue and cry. The hue and cry was a shout loud enough to alert nearby citizens that a crime

Village Violence

Much of village justice among the local inhabitants focused on violence. Violence was endemic in most medieval villages. It was found in the cottage, the fields, and even within the church. The response to violence was somewhat contradictory; it was both wrong and at the same time a regular feature of village society. Violence was a regular part of life partly because too much time was spent in the ale taverns and because of the rampant poverty that sent some men deeply into debt end led them to steal.

The results of spending time in the taverns was drinking too much ale. Meaningless arguments and insults after a night of drinking often ended in acts of violence. Records kept by the local bailiffs, sheriffs, and coroners paint a picture of drunken violence at the taverns and along roads home following an evening at the taverns. According to Joseph and Frances Gies in their book *Daily Life in Medieval Times,* in 1266 the coroner of the village of Bedford, England, recorded that, at about bedtime, three men who had been drinking began quarreling, which led to one man being "stabbed in the heart with a sickle." In another case, also according to the Gieses, four villagers from Wooten, England, who had been drinking were returning home when, according to the coroner, "One with no ulterior motive, turned, drew his bow, and took aim at a man who was following them." Unfortunately, the only woman on the road, "Margery le Wyte, threw her self between the two men and received the arrow in her throat so that she immediately died."

Not all village violence was related to the alehouses. Other common causes of violence, according to bailiffs' reports, were simple disagreements over debts, in one case a halfpenny lent between brothers; trespassing; and thefts of small items such as a sack of flour, a neighbor's hen, or a pie cooling on a window ledge. Yet another court report found in the Gieses' book tells of two brothers who discovered "their sister, Juliana, lying under a haystack with a young man who immediately arose and struck [one of the brothers] on the top of the head, to the brain, with an ax."

had been committed. It might have been "Stop—thief!" or "Help—murder!" Whatever the hue and cry, it was intended to alert the entire village of a crime and to summon help, as this law from the village of Norwich, England, indicates: "When hue-and-cry is raised in the village (day or night) for any felony, a complaint about the crime is to be lodged immediately by men who are subjects of the king, until the person pursued is captured or offers an attachment [promise to appear] for answering the charge in court."[50]

Aside from the town bailiff, responding to criminal activity was primarily the responsibility of the community. Those persons who first responded to the hue and cry were obliged to join with the declarer of the crime in pursuing the criminal, usually to the boundary of the village. Anyone participating in hue and cry had the right to arrest a criminal. In this context, the carrying of arms was permitted, and a criminal violently resisting arrest could be killed with impunity.

Victims of conspicuous crimes such as assaults or rapes might also raise the hue and cry, even if the culprit had escaped, in order to summon those who could witness the effects of the crime. Anyone discovering a corpse was expected to raise the hue and cry immediately, even if the body was cold and pursuit was thus impractical; to fail to do so would have cast suspicion on the "first finder."

Failure to raise the hue and cry, or of the community to respond to it, could result in a neighborhood being fined once the crime was reported to the manorial court. But once it was raised, all able-bodied persons available were obligated to form a posse to pursue the criminal.

The Village Posse

Villagers were sometimes forced to arrest those accused of a crime. The group that came together to track down and arrest criminal suspects was called a *posse,* a Latin term used to describe a group of citizens who are informally granted authority to seize a suspected criminal and to bring him or her to trial. One of the most obvious advantages of the posse in all small villages throughout Europe related to simple economics: Posses did not cost any money.

In most villages, a posse was formed as soon as the hue and cry was uttered by some villager, as this thirteenth-century document attests:

> If they have heard the hue-and-cry raised against such men, that immediately on hearing it they and their household, the

A fifteenth-century painting shows a group of bandits robbing an unsuspecting traveler. Often a village posse was formed to track down such roving criminals.

men of their land being assembled, will follow the trail through their own land and at its boundary show it to the lords of the neighboring lands, that pursuit may thus be made from estate to estate with all diligence until the wrongdoers are apprehended, such pursuit not to end unless some obstacle intervenes, darkness or other reasonable cause.[51]

Once several people established that a crime had been committed and perhaps even determined the identity and whereabouts of the accused, the bailiff or some other person acting under the authority of the lord could order all available citizens to join a posse to find, capture, and bring the accused person back to the village for questioning and possibly a trial.

Posses were generally unarmed farmers or merchants, although sometimes they were poorly armed. Many took simple tools such as pitchforks and shovels to be used as weapons. Others might grab their bows and arrows, but the most common weapon was a simple quarterstaff, a stout stick five to eight feet in length, used as a means of attack and defense. The quarterstaff attained great popularity in Europe when both ends were shod with iron and could be used to beat and subdue an uncooperative suspect.

On occasion, if some sort of violence or criminal activity were anticipated, such as the arrival of a band of vagabonds, the lord might order the bailiff to gather a posse to meet the vagabonds as they entered the village. They might even escort them through town, denying them a place to sleep for the night, or patrol the streets at night in order to discourage the vagabonds from committing crimes. According to historian Frederic L. Cheyette, "There were even women warriors who early in the twelfth century joined a posse of vil-

lagers to attack some mills that she and her fellows claimed were theirs, or the wife of Bernard of Nissan, who took revenge on her husband's enemy when the two men were fighting over a jointly held castle."[52]

Trial by Combat

Once captured by a posse, a suspect's guilt or innocence had to be determined. Crimes with several witnesses were quickly and easily decided by the lord or perhaps by a jury of villagers. Others could be more complicated. One medieval option of determining legal disputes was to resolve them by what was termed trial by combat. Under such circumstances, a suspect hired a champion, or knight-warrior, to fight it out on the battleground with his opponent's champion. The assumption was that God would intervene and decide the case. According to this view, God would not permit the wrong person's champion to win, so trial by combat ensured perfect justice.

Many cases of trial by combat were recorded involving minor squabbles, such as the ownership of a chicken, to far more serious criminal matters. In 1100, in the French village of Saint-Serge, the banks of the Loire River eroded, causing the mills to fail along a certain stretch of the river. Following the erosion, a dispute arose concerning the ownership of the mill property; the conflict involved a man named Engelardus and a monastery of monks.

Unable to resolve the matter, both parties turned to the village lord. According to village records, he went to the river "to inspect the place in question. And, when he was unable to peacefully impose an end to the contentious quarrel, he determined that a judicial battle [duel] ought to be fought." Engelardus and the monks chose champions who agreed to

Poverty sometimes pushed the poor to commit the crime of fleeing from the village to escape mounting debt. Poverty often led to debt that was usually owed to the village lord. Many debtors fell so far behind in their payments, either in kind or in service, that they eventually had no options other than to flee the village to hopefully start a new, debt-free life. Packing up any possessions and secretly abandoning their villages was often the only way to avoid legal action. Many hoped to avoid seizure of what meager personal property they still had, loss of social status for their children, and a life of servitude bordering on slavery.

Flight took many forms. Sons who had the misfortune of not being the firstborn, and thus failed to inherit land upon their father's death, quickly fell into debt. Without land, these sons were forced to saddle their horses, buckle on their armor, and ride off to sell their mercenary services as knights to other nobles at war and in need of mounted soldiers.

Humbler folks were not fortunate enough to own a horse or a suit of armor.

Some villagers, who had lost their land and could not afford to pay taxes or who owned land yet not enough to feed their families, had no choice other than to abandon their property and sell their services working for more fortunate farmers. A writer in the small French town of Tournai, quoted by Michel Mollat in his book *The Poor in the Middle Ages: An Essay in Social History*, commented on fleeing worn-out land: "Just as animals and birds head for soil that is fertile and freshly plowed, and abandon the wasteland, so do mechanics and laborers who live by their toil. For they go where there is a living to be earned . . . and flee places where the people are hobbled by servitude and debt."

As economic conditions worsened, village workers became more desperate. For some, the pressure of poverty was so extreme that the only form of flight that made sense was suicide. Some were so desperate to flee their poverty that they threw themselves into rivers or hanged themselves from the rafters in their homes.

fight a duel to determine the rightful owner of the property. According to the same village account of the trial by combat, Engelardus's champion folded: "God opposes the prideful, so he weakened the champion of Engelardus . . . and Engelardus offered to the monks as a means of concord the entire tithe [ten percent] of the mills and the fish caught there, as well as four deniers in rent from every mill that either existed there now or would exist there in the future."[53]

These sorts of disputes, arising from reasonable disagreements, did not require any penalty beyond the resolution of the dispute.

Other forms of criminal activity, however, involving minor violence, fraudulent deception, and petty theft called for stronger penalties in order to deter such antisocial activities.

The Pillory

Each village had a central public location where the village stocks, also called the village pillory, was used to punish minor violators of local laws. A pillory was a wooden apparatus that clamped around a person's neck and hands, preventing him or her from escaping.

The pillory was used to cause discomfort and humiliation. Petty thieves caught stealing at the marketplace, pickpockets working a Sunday crowd, or merchants caught cheating the public could expect to spend a day in the pillory if caught red-handed. This law in Ipswich, England, provides a warning to butchers: "All butchers should also take care not to display for sale the meat of diseased animals, or that is rotten or smells bad. Any such meat shall be confiscated on the first occasion; on the second occasion the meat shall be confiscated and its seller sent to the pillory."[54]

Pillories were also a form of entertainment for local villagers, who delighted in seeing minor criminals suffering for their crimes. Villagers enjoyed wandering down a street and finding someone clamped and unable to move. Since the offenders could not escape and their faces were exposed, passersby thoroughly enjoyed taunting them with verbal insults as well as pelting them with mud, animal feces, small stones, and dead fish.

Not all criminals were released at the end of the day unscarred by the experience. A cheating butcher or baker might lose business for many weeks, and on occasion a criminal was fastened to a pillory with a nail driven through one ear. At the end of the day, the person's head was released either by removing the nail with a pair of pliers or by tearing the ear from the nail with a quick pull on the head.

Physical Punishment

More serious crimes carried more serious consequences. Crimes such as breaking into homes, stealing family property, or physical violence against other people were dealt with more stridently.

If mysterious circumstances surrounded a crime, punishment might be a dunking in a lake or river until the criminal came close to drowning. However, the worst offenses called for physical injuries such as the loss of a thumb, the branding of the palm of the hand, or removal of an ear. One fifteenth-century medieval source recommended the following punishment for thieves:

Thieves in any man's house in the night, putting him in fear of his life, or breaking up his walls or doors, are burned in the left hand with a hot iron, so that, if they be apprehended again, that mark betrayeth them to have been arraigned of

A medieval manuscript page shows a criminal being executed.

felony before, whereby they are sure at that time to have no mercy.[55]

Justice, as practiced in the medieval village, may not have been as consistently applied as it had been during the Roman Empire, but it worked well nonetheless. Since each village was unique and independent, each was able to apply, live by, and enforce only those laws that were needed by each distinctive village.

The same could be said of most other medieval village institutions. Family life, marriages, work routines, recreation, religion, and finances all reflected the character of the local village. Each of the tens of thousands of medieval villages, which initially took form to provide security and protection for their inhabitants, gradually evolved over many centuries to provide far more than basic protection. As the Middle Ages came to a close after nine hundred years, all of these independent villages began to coalesce to form today's European nations. And as they came together, each made some small contribution to form its nation's identity.

Notes

Introduction: The Emergence of the Medieval Village

1. Quoted in Anne Fermantle, *The Age of Faith.* New York: Time-Life Books, 1965, p. 14.

2. Quoted in Fermantle, *The Age of Faith,* p. 14.

3. Quoted in Frances and Joseph Gies, *Daily Life in Medieval Times.* New York: Black Dog & Leventhal, 1999, p. 126.

4. Quoted in Gies, *Daily Life in Medieval Times,* p. 151.

5. Quoted in University of Pennsylvania, Department of History, *Translations and Reprints from the Original Sources of European History,* vol. 3, no. 5, 1912, p. 42.

Chapter 1: The Village Manor House—Lives of the Nobility

6. Norman Cantor, ed., *The Medieval Reader.* New York: HarperCollins, 1994, pp. 3–4.

7. Quoted in University Pennsylvania, Department of History, *Translations and Reprints from the Original Sources of European History,* vol 4. Philadelphia: University of Pennsylvania Press, 1898, p. 27.

8. Quoted in Frances and Joseph Gies, *Daily Life in a Medieval Village.* New York: Harper & Row, 1990, p. 49.

9. Sherrilyn Kenyon, *The Writer's Guide to Everyday Life in the Middle Ages: The British Isles from 500 to 1500.* Cincinnati: Writer's Digest Books, 1995, p. 56.

10. Quoted in Gies, *Daily Life in Medieval Times,* p. 68.

Chapter 2: The Village Workers

11. Quoted in Steven Alsford, "History of Medieval Maldon," Medieval English Towns. www.trytel.com.

12. Quoted in Graham Nicholson and Jane Fawcett, *The Village in England.* New York: Rizzoli International, 1988, p. 27.

13. Gies, *Daily Life in a Medieval Village,* p. 51.

14. Bernard Knight, "The Medieval Coroner's Duties." Britannia. www.britannia.com.

15. Knight, "The Medieval Coroner's Duties."

16. Steven Alsford, "History of Medieval Ipswich," Medieval English Towns. www.trytel.com.

17. Quoted in Frances and Joseph Gies, *Life in a Medieval Castle.* New York: Harper & Row, 1974, p. 155.

18. Steven Alsford, "History of Medieval Lynn," Medieval English Towns. www.trytel.com.

19. Alsford, "History of Medieval Ipswich."

Chapter 3: A Calendar of Toil

20. Quoted in P.H. Ditchfield, *Old Village Life, or Glimpses of Village Life Throughout All Ages.* New York: E.P. Dutton, 1920, p. 120.

Chapter 4: Family Life in the Cottage

21. Quoted in Michel Mollat, *The Poor in the Middle Ages: An Essay in Social History,* trans. Arthur Goldhammer. New Haven, CT: Yale University Press, 1986, p. 237.

22. Quoted in Gies, *Daily Life in Medieval Times,* p. 166.

23. Quoted in Geneviève D'Haucort, *Life in the Middle Ages,* trans. Veronica Hull. New York: Sun Books, 1963, p. 52.

24. Giovanni della Casa, *Galateo: Of Manners and Behaviours in Familiar Conversation,* trans. Robert Peterson. London: Prive, 1892, p. 47.

25. Quoted in Gies, *Daily Life in Medieval Times,* p. 164.

26. Quoted in Gies, *Daily Life in Medieval Times,* p. 164.

27. Quoted in Alsford, "History of Medieval Lynn."

Chapter 5: Marriage and the Family

28. Quoted in Gies, *Daily Life in Medieval Times,* p. 42.

29. Gies, *Daily Life in Medieval Times,* p. 176.

30. Quoted in Gies, *Daily Life in Medieval Times,* p. 177.

31. Quoted in Werner Rösener, *Peasants in the Middle Ages,* trans. Alexander Stützer. Urbana: University of Illinois Press, 1992, p. 179.

32. Quoted in Rösener, *Peasants in the Middle Ages,* p. 183.

33. Quoted in Gies, *Daily Life in a Medieval Village,* p. 122.

34. Quoted in Gies, *Daily Life in a Medieval Village,* p. 124.

35. Quoted in Gies, *Daily Life in Medieval Times,* p. 183.

36. Quoted in Gies, *Daily Life in Medieval Times,* p. 175.

37. Quoted in Gies, *Daily Life in Medieval Times,* p. 175.

38. Gies, *Daily Life in Medieval Times,* p. 174.

Chapter 6: Relaxation and Enjoyment

39. Kenyon, *The Writer's Guide to Everyday Life in the Middle Ages,* p. 132.

40. Quoted in Roy C. Cave and Herbert H. Coulson, *A Source Book for Medieval Economic History.* New York: Biblo & Tannen, 1965, pp. 150–51.

41. Quoted in Cave and Coulson, *A Source Book for Medieval Economic History,* pp. 107–108.

42. New York Carver, "Soccer Madness in the Middle Ages." www.newyorkcarver.com.

43. Rictor Norton, "Bear-Baiting and Cock-Fighting," *Early Eighteenth-Century Newspaper Reports: A Sourcebook.* www.infopt.demon.co.uk.

44. Medieval English Towns, "Ancient Usages and Customs of the Borough of Maldon." www.trytel.com.

45. Quoted in Gies, *Daily Life in Medieval Times,* p. 170.

Chapter 7: Village Justice

46. Wrenthorpe History Web, "The First Six Hundred Years." www.ejgreen.freeserve.co.uk.

47. Wrenthorpe History Web, "The First Six Hundred Years."

48. Gies, *Daily Life in Medieval Times,* p. 191.

49. Gies, *Daily Life in a Medieval Village,* p. 105.

50. Steven Alsford, "History of Medieval Norwich," *Medieval English Towns.* www.trytel.com.

51. Quoted in Cornell Law, "Bracton on the Laws and Customs of England." http://bracton.law.cornell.edu.

52. Fredric L. Cheyette, *Ermengard of Narbonne and the World of the Troubadours*. Ithaca, NY: Cornell University Press, 2001, p. 241.

53. Paul Halsall, "Charters Relating to Judicial Duels, Eleventh–Twelfth Century," Internet Medieval Sourcebook. www.fordham.edu.

54. Alsford, "History of Medieval Ipswich."

55. EyeWitness, "Crime and Punishment in Elizabethan England." www.ibiscom.com.

For Further Reading

Giovanni della Casa, *Galateo: Of Manners and Behaviours in Familiar Conversation.* Trans. Robert Peterson. London: Prive, 1892. This is one of the more unusual books that provides an account of how people should behave in public. Della Casa lived and wrote during the early sixteenth century, and he freely gives advice on all facets of public behavior.

Geofffry Chaucer, *Canterbury Tales.* Trans. Nevill Coghill. Baltimore: Penguin Classics, 1989. This is the most famous English story from the fourteenth century. It tells the fictional story of twenty-nine travelers who set out for Canterbury on a pilgrimage to the shrine of Saint Thomas Beckett. As each pilgrim tells his or her story, the reader is treated to an extraordinary view of English medieval life.

Anne Fermantle, *The Age of Faith.* New York: Time-Life Books, 1965. This book provides an excellent, readable account of Europe during the Middle Ages. Its focus is on the development of the Christian church and its influence over Europe for one thousand years. Included in the text is an excellent collection of photographs and medieval art.

Thomas Hinde, *The Domesday Book: England's Heritage Then and Now.* London: Coombe Books, 1996. This beautifully illustrated book presents England's geography and heritage from the year 1085, when the first accounting of England's lands was compiled in the Domesday Book. The book provides keys to reading and understanding an entry in the Domesday Book, and the main part of the book is divided into thirty-seven counties.

William Langland, *Piers Plowman.* Trans. A.V.C. Schmidt. London: Oxford University Press, 1992. *Piers Plowman* is a significant literary work for anyone studying the Middle Ages. Although it is an allegorical vision as imagined by Piers, all historians agree that it provides a fascinating and accurate glimpse into mid-fourteenth-century England.

Barbara Tuchman, *A Distant Mirror: The Calamitous Fourteenth Century.* New York: Ballantine Books, 1978. This carefully written book examines daily life during the tragic fourteenth century, which had as its historical backdrop the devastating Black Death that ravaged all of Europe. It is considered one of the great historical novels describing everyday life in medieval Europe for both the peasantry and the nobility.

Jay Williams, *Life in the Middle Ages.* New York: Random House, 1966. This is a slightly aged book yet remains a very well written general work on the Middle Ages. It gives an excellent overview of the period, including one detailed chapter on village life. The book includes a generous offer of medieval art and quotations from primary sources.

Works Consulted

Books

Norman Cantor, ed., *The Medieval Reader*. New York: HarperCollins, 1994. This book contains more than one hundred primary sources from medieval documents.

Roy C. Cave and Herbert H. Coulson, *A Source Book for Medieval Economic History*. New York: Biblo & Tannen, 1965. This work provides a large selection of medieval historical documents that shed light on the lives of people between the eleventh and fourteenth centuries.

Fredric L. Cheyette, *Ermengard of Narbonne and the World of the Troubadours*. Ithaca, NY: Cornell University Press, 2001. Professor of medieval history Fredric L. Cheyette writes a biography of an extraordinary warrior woman, viscountess Ermengard, who gained a following among some inhabitants of the Languedoc region of France during the twelfth century.

Geneviève D'Haucort, *Life in the Middle Ages*. Trans. Veronica Hull. New York: Sun Books, 1963. This work is intended to illuminate the day-to-day activities of the people who lived during the Middle Ages. The author draws from primary sources to describe many of the mundane yet fascinating details and experiences about the lives of both the nobility and the common peasant.

P.H. Ditchfield, *Old Village Life, or Glimpses of Village Life Throughout All Ages*. New York: E.P. Dutton, 1920. This is a dated yet valuable book for insights into the simple lives of villagers throughout Europe during the Middle Ages. The author discusses and describes many local customs of peasant villagers.

Frances and Joseph Gies, *Daily Life in a Medieval Village*. New York: Harper & Row, 1990. This book describes daily life during the Middle Ages, specifically focusing on what it was like to live in a medieval village. Much of the evidence comes from the archaeological work at the village of Elton, England, to help identify the villagers who might have lived there.

——, *Daily Life in Medieval Times*. New York: Black Dog & Leventhal, 1999. This book reproduces much of the work provided by the Gieses in many of their other books. It does, however, provide an excellent cross-section of all social classes in medieval Europe.

——, *Life in a Medieval Castle*. New York: Harper & Row, 1974. This book gives a view of the day-to-day life of people during the Middle Ages, with a specific focus on what it was like to live in a medieval castle.

Sherrilyn Kenyon, *The Writer's Guide to Everyday Life in the Middle Ages: The British Isles from 500 to 1500*. Cincinnati: Writer's Digest Books, 1995. This work provides a general overview of everyday life in medieval Europe, as seen through the eyes of medieval writers.

Michel Mollat, *The Poor in the Middle Ages: An Essay in Social History*. Trans. Arthur Goldhammer. New Haven, CT: Yale University Press, 1986. This is a scholarly work that reports on the plight of the very poor during the Middle Ages. It draws on hundreds of detailed records from village courts and coroners' offices.

Graham Nicholson and Jane Fawcett, *The Village in England*. New York: Rizzoli

International, 1988. This work presents a profile of the history and traditions of village life in late medieval England The depiction of village life is drawn from official town records of more than a dozen small villages.

Anthony Viscount Montague, "A Book of Orders and Rules," *Sussex Archaeological Collections*, vol 7. London: Money Publishing, 1854. This multi-volume set includes a broad range of primary source documentation and descriptions of archaeological artifacts discovered in the county of Sussex, England.

Palladius, *On Husbandrie*. Trans. Barton Lodge. London: N. Trubner, 1873–1879. This fourteenth century book is one of the earliest works to discuss farming techniques and provide practical assistance to new farmers.

Werner Rösener, *Peasants in the Middle Ages*. Trans. Alexander Stützer. Urbana: University of Illinois Press, 1992. This book focuses on peasant life in medieval Germany. The strength of the book is Rösener's in-depth study of social customs in traditional rural family life.

University of Pennsylvania, Department of History, *Translations and Reprints from the Original Sources of European History*. 6 vols. Philadelphia: University of Pennsylvania Press, 1897–1907. The University of Pennsylvania's Department of History selected, translated, and published a large collection of legal documents that provided a glimpse into the lives of medieval people primarily in England, France, and Germany.

Walter of Henley, *Treatise on Husbandry*. Trans. Elizabeth Lamond. London: Longman, Green, 1890. This is one of the few early treatises dedicated to teaching prudent farming techniques to new farmers. The work covers topics such as animals, soils, plowing, seeding, and when to harvest.

Periodicals

University of Pennsylvania, Department of History, *Translations and Reprints from the Original Sources of European History*, vol. 3, no. 5, 1912. This periodical is a scholarly collection of translated medieval documents describing a variety of aspects of medieval life.

Internet Sources

Steven Alsford, "History of Medieval Ipswich," *Medieval English Towns*, www.trytel.com. This is one in a series of historical analyses of several medieval English towns. This one presents the village of Ipswich in a series of documents that portray life in the village.

———, "History of Medieval Lynn," *Medieval English Towns*, www.trytel.com. This is one in a series of historical analyses of several medieval English towns. This one presents the village of Lynn in a series of documents that portray life in the village.

EyeWitness, "Crime and Punishment in Elizabethan England," www.ibiscom. This site contains court documents describing the judicial process in small English villages near the end of the Middle Ages.

Paul Halsall, "Charters Relating to Judicial Duels, Eleventh–Twelfth Century," *Internet Medieval Sourcebook*, www.fordham.edu. Professor Halsall accumulates several medieval documents describing different types of duels fought to resolve judicial disputes.

Bernard Knight, "The Medieval Coroner's Duties," *Britannia*, www.britannia.com. This site presents a large number of coroner reports that depict his duties and provide interesting insights into death in medieval villages.

New York *Carver*, "Soccer Madness in the Middle Ages," www.newyorkcarver.com. This site presents the early history of soccer and some of the more bizarre aspects of the early game.

Rictor Norton, "Bear-Baiting and Cock-Fighting," *Early Eighteenth-Century Newspaper Reports: A Sourcebook,* www.infopt.demon.co.uk. This site presents newspaper articles written about bear-baiting during the Middle Ages.

Wrenthorpe History Web, "The First 600 years," www.ejgreen.freeserve.co.uk. A detailed account of the first 600 years of the village of Wrenthorpe, England as told by court, church, and coroner records.

Websites

Britannia (www.britannia.com). This website is an excellent repository of authoritative information on major topics in English history.

Calvin College (www.calvin.edu). The Calvin College website not only provides students and faculty with links to all departments but also to various research projects, including research about the Middle Ages.

Early Eighteenth-Century Newspaper Reports: A Sourcebook (www.infopt. demon.co.uk). This site provides dozens of interesting newspaper articles from various English newspapers. The articles describe a variety of unusual and fascinating activities during the late Middle Ages.

EyeWitness—History Through the Eyes of Those Who Lived It (www.ibis com.com). This awarding-winning website provides a broad sweep of eyewitness accounts from many major historical events.

Geoffrey Chaucer Page (http://icg.fas.har vard.edu). This website provides all of Chaucer's works as well as interlinear translations.

Internet Medieval Sourcebook (www.ford ham.edu). The Internet Medieval Sourcebook is maintained by Fordham University and is organized by three main index pages, with a number of supplementary documents. Each section contains dozens of primary sources covering an array of political, social, and economic topics.

Medieval English Towns (www.trytel.com). This website provides a fascinating history of several medieval villages in England. It provides a map of the villages, an appendix of the laws governing them, and general discussions of the villages' buildings, bridges, and economy.

New York Carver (www.newyorkcarver.com). This website provides a wide variety of stories on the Middle Ages, discussing architecture, art, and various cultural activities.

Poet's Corner (www.geocities.com). This website provides 6,700 selected poems written in English by 780 poets, including several poems from the middle ages.

Wrenthorpe History Web (www.ejgreen. freeserve.co.uk). This small website provides a brief history of the village of Wrenthorpe, England, during the Middle Ages.

Index

accounting, 26
agriculture, 36–45
animals, 18, 36, 41, 44–45, 72–73
archery, 71

bailiff, 26–27, 75
baker, 30–32
bearbaiting, 72–73
blacksmith, 34–35
Bracton, Henri de, 12
bread, 30–32, 47
butcher, 32–34

calving, 44–45
    see also livestock
Cantor, Norman, 16
Casa, Giovanni della, 51
cattle, 44–45
    see also livestock
Cave, Roy C., 71
Chapelot, Jean, 10
charters, 67
Cheyette, Frederic L., 81
childbirth, 59–60
child labor, 55, 62
church. See religion
cleanliness, 46–47, 50–51
clothing, 51–52
College, Calvin, 23
combat, 81–82
cooking, 15
cottages, 46–47, 48, 52–54
Coulson, Herbert C., 71
courts of law, 76–77
crime, 77–84
crops, 36, 40

Daily Life in Medieval Times (Gies), 65, 78, 79
dancing, 74
D'Haucourt, Geneviève, 51

diet. *See* eating; food; meals
disease, 53
*Distant Mirror: The Calamitous Fourteenth
    Century, A* (Tuchman), 38

eating, 14, 15, 20–21
    see also food
entertainment, 68–75
epidemics, 53
"Extracts from the Halmote Court Rolls
    of the Prior and Convent of Durham,
    1345–83" (College), 23

families, 46–55
    see also ladies; lords; nobility; villagers
famine, 50
    see also poverty
farming, 36–45
flails, 41
food
    bread baking, 32
    milk, 54–55
    nobility and, 14, 15–16
    preparation of, 15, 44
    preservation of, 44
    types of, 20–21
    villagers and, 47–49
Fossier, Robert, 10
funerals, 64

Galateo (Casa), 51
Gies, Frances and Joseph, 27, 57, 65,
    78, 79
Glower, John, 48–49
Great Peasant Revolt, the, 38
gristmills, 30

harrowing, 39
harvesting, 40
haying, 42

"Haymaker's Song, The," 43
health, 53
herbs, 53
hue and cry, 78–80
hunting, 23–24
hygiene, 50–51

illness, 53
inheritance, 58
ironworkers, 35

jousting, 70–71
justice, 23, 32

Kenyon, Sherrilyn, 19, 66
kings, 18
knights, 22–23, 70

ladies, 18–20
land ownership, 58
Langland, William, 46
laws, 23, 32, 34
Life in a Medieval Village (Gies), 27
Life in the Middle Ages (D'Haucourt), 51
Lives of the Saints (Meidenhod), 53–54
livestock, 18, 36, 41, 44–45, 54–55
lords, 16–18

manners, 51
manor house, 14–16
Master of the Game, The, 24
meals, 14, 15, 20–21, 51
    see also eating; food
meat, 32–34
medicine, 53
Medieval Reader, The (Cantor), 16
Meidenhod, Hali, 53–54
Middle Ages, 8–9, 10–12, 84
midwives, 60
milkmaids, 54–55
miller, 29–30
mills, 29–30
millstones, 30
Mollat, Michael, 82

nobility
    children of, 20–22
    daily life of, 14–16
    duties of, 18–20
    education of, 20, 22–23
    hunting and, 23–24, 77
    manners of, 21
    power of, 17–28
    servants of, 14–16, 62
    uprisings against, 38
    see also kings; ladies; lords

parsons, 62
Pastoureaux, 38
Paul the Deacon, 10
peasants. *See* farming; villagers; specific
    names of jobs
pilgrimages, 16
pillories, 82–83
planting, 38–40, 41
plowing, 36–38, 41
poaching, 77
*Poor in the Middle Ages: An Essay in Social
    History, The* (Mollat), 82
porridge, 47–48
posses, 80–82
pottage, 47–48
poverty, 46–47, 50, 82
priests, 62
punishments, 81–84

rebellions, 38
record keeping, 28
reeves, 27–29
religion
    baptism of babies, 60
    nobility and, 14
    pilgrimages and, 16
    power of, 66–67
    priests' work and, 62
    revolts, 38
Richard II (king of England), 38
Robin Hood, 77
Roman Empire, 8–10

Romans, Humbert de, 71

sanitation, 46–47
   see also hygiene
scythe, 40
servants, 14–16, 62
sheep, 44–45
   see also livestock
sickle, 40
sickness, 53
smoking (of meat), 44
soccer, 68–70
Source Book for Medieval Economic
   History, A (Cave and Coulson), 71
sports, 68–73
squire, 22
starvation, 50
stealing, 77–78
steward, 25–26
stocks, 32

table manners, 20–21, 51
tally stick, 28
taverns, 74–75
Tertullian, 9–10
thieving, 77–78
threshing, 40–42
tools
   counting sticks, 28
   eating utensils, 20, 49–50
   farming, 35, 36, 37, 39–41, 42–43
   household, 35, 48, 50, 54
   medical, 53
Tour, Geoffrey de la, 57
Treatise on Husbandry (Walter of Henley),41
trial by combat, 81–82
Tuchman, Barbara, 38

uprisings, 38

village
   business dealings in, 26–29

corruption in, 26, 27, 28–29, 30, 32
description of, 12–13, 25
economic structure of, 56
jobs in, 25–35
justice in, 76–84
law enforcement in, 26–29
management in, 25–29
marketplaces of, 67–68
rules for, 67
social structure of, 12, 56
Village and the House in the Middle Ages,
   The (Chapelot and Fossier), 10
villagers
   bathing and, 51
   childbirth and, 59–60
   children of, 49, 55, 60–61
   clothing of, 51–52
   cooking and, 49
   death and, 64
   health of, 53
   homes of, 46–47, 48
   housework and, 52–54
   hunting and, 39
   inheritance and, 58, 64–65
   land ownership and, 58
   marriage and, 56–59
   meals of, 47–50
   medicines of, 53
   old age and, 62–64
   poverty and, 46–47, 82
   social activities of, 67, 68, 73–74
   widowhood and, 65
violence, 79
   see also entertainment; sports
Vitry, Jacques de, 38

Walter of Henley, 18, 36, 41
water, 47
water jousting, 70–71
weddings, 58–59
Writer's Guide to Everyday Life in the
   Middle Ages (Kenyon), 66

Picture Credits

Cover Image: © Scala/Art Resource, NY
© Archivo Iconografico, S.A./CORBIS, 28, 31, 33
© Bettmann/CORBIS, 46
© Fine Art Photographic Library, London/Art Resource, NY, 12
© Giraudon/Art Resource, NY, 15, 19, 39, 42, 49, 57, 60, 61, 70, 76, 78, 83
© Hulton Archive, 8, 55
© Erich Lessing/Art Resource, NY, 22, 65, 73, 75
© Gianni Dagli Orti/CORBIS, 37
© The Pierpont Morgan Library/Art Resource, NY, 18, 45
© Reunion des Musees Nationaux/Art Resource, NY, 17, 52
© Scala/Art Resource, NY, 66, 69, 80
© Snark/Art Resource, NY, 26, 34, 63
© Gustavo Tomsich/CORBIS, 25

About the Author

James Barter received his undergraduate degree in history and classics at the University of California at Berkeley, followed by graduate studies in ancient history and archaeology at the University of Pennsylvania. Mr. Barter has taught history as well as Latin and Greek.

A Fulbright scholar at the American Academy in Rome, Mr. Barter worked on archaeological sites in and around the city as well as on sites in the Naples area. Mr. Barter also has worked and traveled extensively in Greece.

Mr. Barter currently lives in Rancho Santa Fe, California, with his seventeen-year-old daughter, Kalista, who is a student at Torrey Pines High School, works as a soccer referee, and is in a quandary about colleges. Mr. Barter's older daughter, Tiffany, is married, teaches violin, and has a business arranging live classical music performances.